MACKINTOSH'S MASTERWORK

MACKINTOSH'S □□ THE GLASGOW
MASTERWORK □□ SCHOOL OF ART

▪ *EDITOR* ▪

WILLIAM BUCHANAN

Chambers

CHAMBERS
An imprint of Larousse plc
43–45 Annandale Street
Edinburgh, EH7 4AZ

This paperback edition first published by Chambers 1994
First published as a hardback by Richard Drew Publishing Ltd 1989

10 9 8 7 6 5 4 3 2 1

A CIP catalogue record for this book is available from
the British Library

ISBN 0 550 22570 6

The publisher acknowledges a subsidy from the Scottish Arts Council
towards the cost of colour printing

Designed by James W Murray
Front cover illustrations: Hugh C S Ferguson measured drawing,
pen and ink, 45 x 97 cm, of Glasgow School of Art North Façade, 1961;
'Rosebud' stained-glass motifs from doors in the School of Art and
bookcase from the Mackintosh Collection
Set in Korinna and Caslon by Swains (Glasgow) Ltd
Colour reproduction by Swains (Edinburgh) Ltd
Monochrome reproduction by Butler and Tanner Ltd, Frome, Somerset
Printed in Singapore by C S Graphics Pte Ltd

CONTENTS

ACKNOWLEDGEMENTS

We are deeply honoured that Eckart Muthesius agreed to write a Foreword to this book. In addition we are grateful to him for allowing us to quote from letters between Mackintosh and his father, Hermann Muthesius.

To the former Governors of the School and their then Chairman Dr William Leggat Smith, CBE, MC, we gratefully acknowledge permission to quote from the minutes of the meetings of their predecessors. Sadly, this book was written as the composition of the Board of Governors, with representatives of local and professional bodies, introduced in 1892, was coming to an end. We thank David Walker, a Governor at that time, for his help in the initial stages of this publication.

We would like to thank the Hunterian Art Gallery, University of Glasgow, Mackintosh Collection, for permission to quote from Mackintosh's lecture notes, and also the Curator, Pamela Robertson, for her help. We owe a debt to Keppie Henderson, Architects (now S B T Keppie Ltd, and once Honeyman, Keppie & Mackintosh) for allowing us to quote from their job-books. Brian Blench, past Keeper of Decorative Arts, Glasgow Art Gallery & Museum, also deserves our gratitude.

We thank former Director, Thomas Pannell (now retired); former School Secretary and Treasurer, Frank Kean MBE (now retired); former Assistant Secretary (Buildings), Drew Perry (now retired); Senior Lecturer in Architectural Science, Dr Alec James; Principal Librarian, Ian Monie; former Architectural Librarian, Neil McVicar; and other members of staff for extra demands on their services. Other essential help is deeply appreciated from Marion Breen, Barbara and Murray Grigor, Professor Anthony Jones, Duncan McAra, Anne Robin, Marjorie Thau, and Soichiro Tsukamoto. Herr Muthesius's text was translated from German by Phil Goddard of Lesley Bernstein Translations, London.

This book is the work of various people who were, at the time of its original publication in hardback, members of staff of the Glasgow School of Art. They are: William Buchanan, former Head of the School of Fine Art (now retired); Dr James Macaulay, Senior Lecturer, History of Architecture, the Mackintosh School of Architecture; Professor Andrew MacMillan, former Head of the Mackintosh School of Architecture (now retired); George Rawson, Fine Art Librarian; Mike Strang, former Computer Technician; Peter Trowles, Taffner Curator of the Mackintosh Collection. The index was produced by Christine McGeoch, former Assistant (Academic Services). The book was designed by James Murray, Lecturer in the Graphic Design & Illustration Department. The measured drawings of furniture were by former students Ian MacDonald and Jeremy Ashley.

There is often a gap between looking and seeing, and a much larger gap between seeing and understanding. This book is the result of a great deal of looking at the School with the intention of seeing and understanding what its creator not only did, but also meant. Without the enthusiasm and patience of Richard Drew, it would have been impossible for the contributors to cope with the usual academic demands of their posts and, like good students, produce their essays, almost, on time.

William Buchanan

1
Photographer unknown
■□ HERMANN MUTHESIUS
Taken between 1896 and 1903 while
Muthesius was at the German Embassy in
London. He was Technical Attaché, and later
combined this with the post of Cultural
Attaché
Eckart Muthesius

2
Mihya-Diez Dührkoop
□■ ECKART MUTHESIUS WITH HIS MOTHER,
1910
Photograph, early colour process
Taken in Berlin. Eckart aged six
Eckart Muthesius

3
Francis Newbery
□□ ANNA MUTHESIUS SEWING, c. 1902
■ A study, reproduced on the cover of *Jugend*,
no 33, 1904, for a larger work since
destroyed. Present location unknown
Eckart Muthesius

FOREWORD

THOUGHTS ON MY GODFATHER

ECKART
MUTHESIUS

BERLIN

We are delighted that the godson of Charles Rennie Mackintosh, Eckart Muthesius – himself a distinguished architect and designer – was willing to contribute a Foreword. This pleasure was doubled when we discovered later that Herr Muthesius's other godfather was the Head of the Glasgow School of Art and a staunch supporter of Mackintosh's genius, Francis Newbery. He was, therefore, a link with the two principal characters in the story of the building of the School of Art. His friendship with the Newbery family was a treasured memory. 'They gave me so much during the time when I was a young man.'

Herr Muthesius's father, Hermann Muthesius, perhaps 'the only person who adequately understood what was going on [in architecture] in Britain in the last quarter of the nineteenth century'[1] obviously had a special relationship with Mackintosh. In the letters to him, now in the Hunterian Art Gallery of Glasgow University, Mackintosh speaks frankly, as to a trusted friend. In pride of place, on the mantelshelf above the fire in their superb white living-room the Mackintoshes placed two SURIMONO — *Japanese prints — objects for contemplation and inspiration. They were a present from Muthesius and his wife Anna.*

Sadly Eckart Muthesius died in July 1989 just before the publication of this book.

There are several possible reasons why Hermann Muthesius had such an affinity with Mackintosh.

The art of space, the house as a work of art, architecture as an ideal: all these concepts were central to Muthesius's cultural philosophy. They help to explain why it was that Muthesius looked so favourably on Mackintosh and appreciated his consistent, artist's approach to interior design. To Mackintosh, an artist's outlook involved creativity and inventiveness on the one hand, and form which did not neglect meaning on the other. Because this outlook was reflected in his practical applications of functional designs for living spaces, his contemporaries often did not understand him. It was the creative skill, the principle which pointed at something beyond the purely utilitarian, which Muthesius admired in Mackintosh. And this was why Mackintosh was asked to be my godfather, strengthening the artistic and family ties which already existed.

Hermann Muthesius always advocated a domestic architecture in which the prime criterion was its functional purpose, though he was not afraid to claim a high degree of aesthetic sensibility. In Mackintosh, he saw a much closer reflection of the need for quality, artistry and functionalism than in the work of other contemporary architects such as Voysey. But Muthesius knew that Mackintosh's interior designs were not easily reconciled with everyday utility. He made the following inevitable comment in his book, published in 1904, *Das englische Haus:*

> We should also ask ourselves whether this kind of intensity is appropriate for everyday interiors. Mackintosh's interiors achieve a level of sophistication which is way beyond the lives of even the artistically educated section of the population. The refinement and austerity of the artistic atmosphere prevailing here does not reflect the ordinariness that fills so much of our lives. A single book with the wrong type of cover lying on the table would spoil the effect; indeed, even an ordinary person, especially an ordinary man, would look out of place wearing his simple working clothes in this fairytale world. At least for the time being, it is hard to imagine that aesthetic culture will prevail so much in our lives that interiors like these will become commonplace. But they are paragons created by a genius, to show humanity that there is something higher in the distance which transcends everyday reality.

He was also aware of the disapproval of architectural critics of the time, such as Adolf Loos, who strongly questioned the late-nineteenth-century idea of interiors whose perfection of form made them self-contained works of art. The point under discussion was the danger of taking an over-aesthetic approach. As we have seen, Muthesius was just as unwilling to take this approach himself, but he could not ignore Mackintosh's highly exacting principles and almost visionary creative impulse.

It was this combination which led him to promote Mackintosh's work on the continent. Even before he introduced Mackintosh in *Das englische Haus*, it is possible that he first acted as a 'middleman' for him in 1898. This was the year in which Mackintosh received his first foreign commission, an interior for a dining room, from the Munich publisher H. Bruckmann, who described it in his magazine *Die Kunst*.

The role Muthesius played in 1903 is well documented. This was the year in which the architect Alfred Grenander asked Muthesius to put him in contact with Mackintosh. Soon afterwards Mackintosh designed a dining room for the Berlin industrial art company A. S. Ball, which was holding an interior design exhibition organised by Grenander.[2] Between 1898 and 1905 Mackintosh ventured outside Scotland with international commissions in 1900, 1901, and 1902. The most important of these was in Vienna, where he designed his own room for the Secession Exhibition of 1900 and a music salon for the banker Fritz Warndörfer and his wife. His work in Austria seems, more than elsewhere, to have given Mackintosh opportunities to discuss with others the ideas of compression of form. It is quite possible that he met Josef Hoffmann and Adolf Loos in Vienna. Both of these used more solid shapes than Mackintosh and defined objects in a more decisive way, but their work was not dissimilar to his own.

But there was no exchange of influences in Germany. Neither van de Velde, who was working with a similarly exacting concept of individual space, nor Bernhard Pankok and others of their contemporaries, left any mark on the Scotsman. The German press, nevertheless, followed Mackintosh's work with great interest from very early on: it was discussed in art journals, and in 1901 his competition entry for the *Haus eines Kunstfreundes* was featured in *Innendekoration*. Although this design was never built, today it is regarded as one of his best. At the time, all he received was a consolation prize. Mackintosh's entry was not in the running because he was less interested in the need for perspective representation than in the delicate, careful structuring of space. Following his participation in the Dresden Applied Arts Exhibition in the same year, he achieved considerable success at the 1902 Exhibition of Decorative Art in Turin. This gained him a place in exhibitions in Moscow and Budapest, though in Turin all he won was an honorary award. Muthesius had expected greater things; he would have liked to have seen Mackintosh winning a Grand Prix so that he gained the international recognition he deserved.

No one expresses better than Mackintosh what a pillar of moral support Muthesius was to him. 'I am afraid that there is little chance for us, getting a Grand Prix at Torino, but when you say we should have it — we feel that we have got something we value much more.'[3]

NOTES

[1] Dennis Sharp 'Mackintosh and Muthesius' in Patrick Nuttgens (ed.), *Mackintosh and his Contemporaries*, Murray, 1988, p. 15. See also N. Jopek, 'Mackintosh und Muthesius', *Jahrbuch der Hamburger Kunstsammlungen*, vol. 24, 1979, pp. 151-8.

[2] See the correspondence between Muthesius and Mackintosh in the West Berlin Werkbundarchiv, 12 May 1903.

[3] op. cit., 1902.

MACKINTOSH : NEWBERY AND THE BUILDING OF THE SCHOOL

WILLIAM BUCHANAN

AT the beginning of 1914 Francis Newbery painted a portrait of Charles Mackintosh, showing the forty-five-year-old architect grasping the plans of the School of Art. Mackintosh is hardly recognisable as the dashing figure photographed by J. Craig Annan about twenty years earlier. His face is now chubby, his eyes anxious, his mouth set. He is at the end of a prodigiously fertile period during which he had produced the major part of his work, but both time and trouble have clearly overtaken him. He was having difficulties coping with his work. In June, later that year, his partnership in the firm of Honeyman, Keppie & Mackintosh was to be dissolved, and some time after the outbreak of the First World War in August, he and his wife Margaret would leave Glasgow. Newbery made a record of his friend at a bleak time in his life.

Newbery was the invigorating head of the School of Art. Mackintosh had been the School's talented student and then, at twenty-eight, the brilliant architect of its new building. Mackintosh created for Newbery and for generations of art students in Glasgow, not only one of the most exciting buildings in which to study, but also a landmark in architectural history. The School was to be a life's work for Newbery; for Mackintosh it was to be his masterwork.

The School, founded in 1844, moved in 1869 to the south-east corner of a block of buildings overlooking Sauchiehall Street and Rose Street. In the centre of this block stood the city's Art Gallery. Although the School's accommodation — once dwelling houses — was cramped, it ranked high in National Competitions. In 1885, the year Newbery arrived, it came third, after Birmingham and Lambeth. Chas R. McIntosh, as he then spelt his name, aged fifteen, first appeared on the School's register in September 1883. His

4
Francis Newbery
CHARLES R. MACKINTOSH, 1914
Oil, 110.5 × 61.4 cm
'It unmistakably portrays a figure familiar in the great seminary on Garnethill,' *Glasgow Herald*, 14 February 1914
Scottish National Portrait Gallery, Edinburgh

5
Charles R. Mackintosh
AN ANTIQUE RELIEF, c. 1886
Sepia, 72.7 × 54.7 cm
A detail from a cast listed as Apollodonus's
Boy and Griffin with Ornament
Hunterian Art Gallery, University of Glasgow,
Mackintosh Collection

father's occupation is shown as clerk although he was a policeman. William McIntosh (who retained this spelling of his surname) was a clerk in the Chief Constable's office where he served for forty-one years rising to the rank of Superintendent but known as the Chief Clerk. Charles, the second son in a family of eleven, was given as a middle name the maiden name of his mother.

Mackintosh spent his days in the office of John Hutchison and evenings at the School of Art. There he embarked on the National Course of Instruction for Government Schools of Art.[1] Curiously, Mackintosh tackled first the Painting Course, in session 1884-5, Stage 11, Painting ornament from the flat, and in the next session Stage 12, Painting ornament from the cast. His *An Antique Relief* (University of Glasgow) could be used as a good example of the product of this course. On the Drawing Course he progressed from Stage 1, Linear Drawing with instruments, sub-section a) Geometry, as far as Stage 5, Shading from the round, sub-section b) From cast of ornament. The School placed great importance on drawing. The Chairman said at a meeting in 1885:

> All our great industries — whether of ship-building or house building, whether of engineering or machine making, whether of pattern-making or the higher art of painting — must first have their origin in drawing, and without this basis none of them can be established. The shipbuilder must first design his model; the architect his structure; the engineer his railway, his docks, or his bridges; the painter, his sketch; and the designer his ideal, before he can begin his operations.

It was not until Mackintosh's fourth year, 1886-7, that there is evidence of formal architectural education — it seems to have been a local course — when he passed Elementary Architecture. In his fifth year he passed Building Construction, and won one of the five bronze medals which came to Glasgow, for his Mountain Chapel. This, part of the Science & Art scheme, was at Stage 23, Applied design, Technical studies, sub-section b) Architectural Design. As a medal winner perhaps this drawing was exhibited with the others in what are now Rooms 100 and 101 in the Victoria & Albert Museum. The next session, 1888-9, he completed a section of the Modelling Course, Stage 18, Modelling ornament sub-section a) From the cast. He was awarded a National Queen's Prize for his set of Designs for a Presbyterian Church (sub-section 23b). In 1890 he carried off the Alexander Thomson Travelling Scholarship. The session 1890-1 brought him a Silver Medal for both the design for a Public Hall and the design for a Science and Art Museum (sub-section 23b). Then in 1891-2 came his Gold Medal for a Chapter House (sub-section 23b again).

Mackintosh's teacher of architecture — there was only one to begin with — was Thomas Smith.[2] In the session 1889-90 an assistant was appointed and the fine draughtsman Alexander McGibbon, who later joined the staff, became visiting master. In 1891-2 a group of Glasgow heavyweights became visitors: William Leiper, W. F. Salmon, J. J. Burnet, J. A. Campbell, and John Keppie. Mackintosh would know the latter for he had joined the firm of Honeyman & Keppie in 1889. That year Honeyman & Keppie entered three schemes for the competition for the city's new Art Gallery and Museum, which was to include a new Art School. One of these schemes was drawn entirely by Mackintosh. His plan[3] shows a lecture theatre with seating arranged to face a speaker placed in a corner, a layout which he was to use in the School which he did build.

Mackintosh left the School at the end of the session 1893-4. He had spent ten years part-time there and he had received a broad education which served him well. He must also have known the School's problems intimately.

It was September 1892 when the Governors applied to the Bellahouston Bequest Fund for help which included a grant for 'a special building, fitted with modern requirements — say £15,000 or £20,000'. Eventually, in March 1894 an encouraging reply was received, so the spaces in the School and in its studio at 162 Bath Street were measured. An estimate for a building was calculated and a price was obtained for a piece of open ground in Renfrew Street. In January 1895 the Governors were offered £10,000 for 'a plain build-

6

Honeyman & Keppie
COMPETITION FOR GLASGOW ART
GALLERY & MUSEUM, 1891·2
From the *British Architect,* 10 June 1892.
Mackintosh laid out on the left of the plan
rooms for the Antique, Ornament,
Landscape, Architecture, Modelling, Design
Mitchell Library, Glasgow

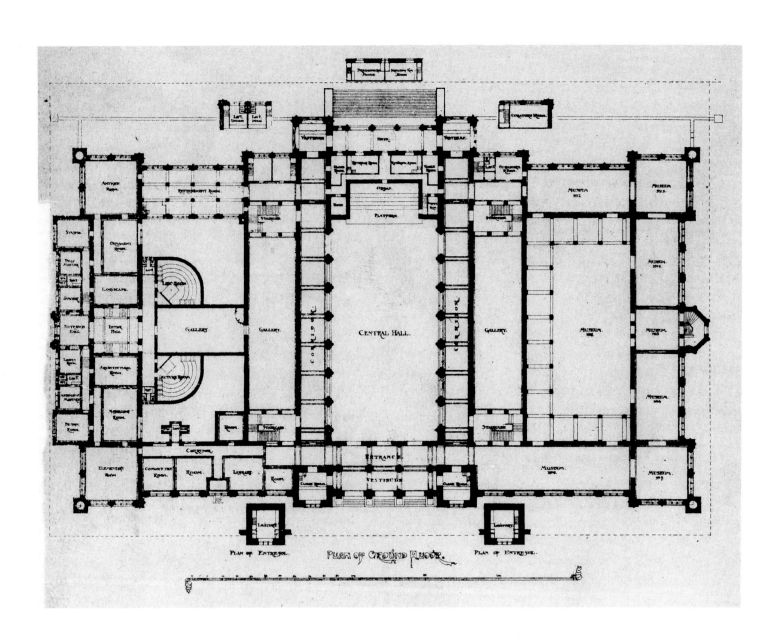

ing affording accommodation equal to that at present in service'. The sum of £6000 was to be for the purchase of the site, with £4000 in cash. A condition of this grant was that the Governors would raise £6000.

By March 1896 a total of £21,000 had been raised. Calculating £1 then to be worth £42 today[4] this would amount to £882,000. Some of the Governors made personal donations. James Fleming, the Chairman, gave £250 (£10,500) and Sir Renny Watson £100 (£4200). Commerce in the city helped: Templeton the carpet-makers contributed £250; the *Glasgow Herald* sent £100; and the shipping magnates Burrell & Sons added a modest £20 (£840). The Corporation of Glasgow donated £5600 (£235,200), and the Scottish Education Department gave £1500 (£63,000). It was agreed to go ahead with a limited competition for a building costing £14,000 (£588,000). There would be no prizes but the winner would receive 5 per cent of the cost of the building.

Newbery drew up draft Conditions of the Competition and a block plan. A Building Committee was appointed with Fleming as its Convenor. The Assessors, Sir James King and Sir Renny Watson, were given powers to co-opt. By May Newbery had completed the schedules. Thomas Armstrong, Director of the Art Division at the South Kensington Museum, gave them his general approval — this was necessary because the School then was part of the educational system run by them — as did Mr Macmath, the Property Surveyor of the School Board of Glasgow. In June the Competition Conditions were ready (p. 205), based on standards laid out in the Department of Science & Art's *Directory* (revised to June 1895). From this came the conditions that windows should not have mullions and small panes, that top-lit rooms should be ceiled to the rafters, that tie beams and roof timbering should not be used, that all class-rooms should, as far as possible, communicate with each other directly, that the staircase should be at the centre of the building, and that rooms should be ventilated by shafts carried above the roof. The standard formula for Antique Room windows, i.e. three-quarters of the depth of the room, was adopted by Newbery

but he stipulated that the windows should be square headed and should run the length of the room. He suggested the floor on which each room was to be positioned. The options were very constrained by a tight brief and long narrow site.

In August the competitors wrote jointly to say that they had found it impossible to build what was specified for the sum of £14,000. They suggested that they would indicate which part of their plans could be carried out for the given sum. The Governors protested 'it is but a plain building that is required'. The architects replied that they 'understood that the building must be of great simplicity and plainness' and they reminded the Governors that not only was it a large school and on a steep gradient, but that their own Conditions stated that any building costing 10 per cent above the budget would automatically be excluded. The Governors could only capitulate. The deadline for the submission of plans was put back from 15 September to 1 October.

In December the Assessors reported that they had selected a set of drawings. They had also sent all the drawings for consideration by the Director of Art at the South Kensington Museum and the Director of the Science Museum. The latter, R. F. Festing, a Major-General in the Royal Engineers, was doubtless interested in matters of construction. These men had approved the same set of drawings. Writing on 17 November 1896 they stated that the building would be 'better than any that could be obtained from the other designs'. The Assessors suggested that instead of the centre section indicated on the plans as that which could be built for £14,000, the section from the east wall, as far west as funds would allow, should be built. At the Governors' meeting on 13 January 1897 it was reported that a frontage of 153 ft could be built within budget. The Chairman then opened the envelope marked with three wishbones, which corresponded to the wishbones on the plans, and drew out the name of Honeyman & Keppie as winners. Honeyman & Keppie replied from 140 Bath Street accepting the commission. Although none of the competition submissions has been found it is unlikely that the winning plans would have needed a distinguishing mark for they would have been so different from

7
OS Map, Sheet VI. 10. 4
LANARKSHIRE,
GLASGOW AND ITS ENVIRONS, 1896
This detail shows the School and the site for
the new building

Glasgow Room, Mitchell Library

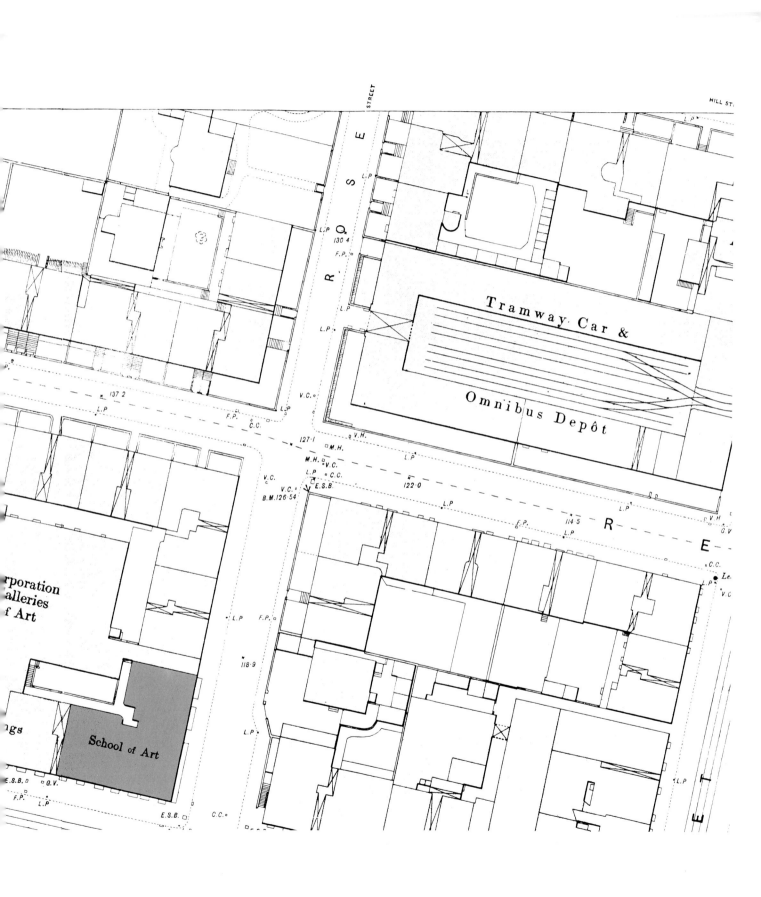

STREET

HILL ST

R

S

O

S

E

130·4

L.P

F.P.

L.P

L.P

Tramway Car &

Omnibus Depôt

137·2

V.C.

L.P

F.P.

C.C.

V.H.

127·1

M.H.

L.P

M.H.

V.C.

V.C.

L.P

C.C.

122·0

114·5

R

V.C.

L.P

E.S.B.

E

B.M.126·54

F.P.

G.V

L.P

rporation

alleries

f Art

L.P

F.P.

L.P

C.C.

118·9

L.P

L.P

gs

School of Art

E.S.B.

G.V.

V.C.

F.P.

L.P

L.P

E.S.B.

C.C.

E

those of the other competitors.

While Newbery, as Headmaster, would rightly have had a large say in this decision, these facts must end the legend that it was solely at Newbery's insistence, and against bitter opposition, that Mackintosh won this competition. Do they prove that Mackintosh's design was, without doubt, the best? The answer seems, overwhelmingly, yes, given that the written record is a true one. Yet one question needs an answer, and that is how such a radical building was accepted without someone, such as Newbery, promoting it forcefully?

All the competition designs were on view in February 1897 in the Corporation Galleries. Mackintosh's designs would certainly have exasperated the Glasgow architectural establishment for no other reason than it is the nature of establishments to oppose the new. The local newspapers gave scant notice, remarking that the entrance was in the centre of the building and missing the whole subtle, balanced asymmetry of the façade. The *Glasgow Herald* thought that the 'practical requirements of the School have dominated the style of the building' not realising that this was one of the fresh ideas expressed in the building which had been designed from the inside out.

In December the tenders were accepted and the start of work was sanctioned. Mackintosh gave the Governors almost exactly what they had specified. The large studio windows are the result of the given formula: the studios, 35 ft in depth, have windows 26 ft above the floor. The first plan follows the brief closely but the need to build in two stages resulted in later changes: the library rose to the first floor and the lecture theatre sank to the basement. Mackintosh had been asked to provide a plain building and that is what he did — although, in another sense, it is an immensely rich one.

Is it possible to deduce some of the thoughts running through Mackintosh's richly fertile mind as he created the School?

There was his fundamental belief that art, architecture and the crafts were one creative whole. His education had taught him this and had also equipped him to create at least one work quite literally with his own hands for he modelled, full size, for the stone carvers the roundel above the entrance to the School.

There was Mackintosh's great love of Scottish architecture. When he gave a talk, 'Scotch Baronial Architecture',[5] to the Glasgow Architectural Association in 1891, he used such phrases as 'dear to my heart' and 'deep and filial affection'. He described how some will go along 'muddy roads and

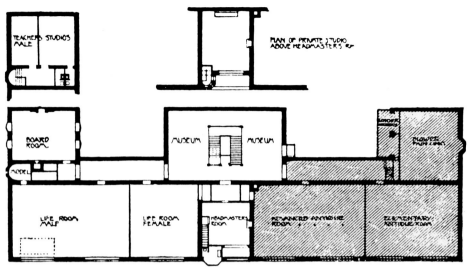

COMPLETE PLANS OF THE
GLASGOW SCHOOL OF ART

FIRST FLOOR PLAN

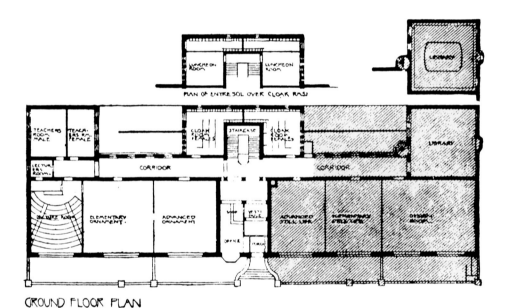

GROUND FLOOR PLAN

THE SHADED PORTION
IS NOT BUILT

BASEMENT FLOOR PLAN

10
FLOOR PLANS
From the Prospectus, 1907-8

snowy path, and with glowing heart but shivering hand . . . sketch . . . the . . . venerable castle with feelings of the most indescribable delight'. One of his two drawings of Maybole Castle in Ayrshire (1895, University of Glasgow) shows an unusual oriel window set on corbelling. This may have inspired the design of the window at the bottom of the tower on the east façade of the School. Mackintosh also knew, at first hand, traditional English buildings. In 1894 he sketched in Somerset, Devon and Gloucestershire, and the next year in Dorset and again in Somerset.

There was also in Mackintosh's mind the history of architecture. His Silver Medal was gained for exercises in the Early Classic and the French Renaissance styles, his Gold for the Italian Renaissance. He got no award for his Gothic, a railway station. It was an Early Classic which won him the Alexander Thomson Travelling Scholarship enabling him to see something of Europe. He visited art galleries and filled sketchbooks with drawings of buildings in Italy. In Venice he was so moved by the Ducal palace that he feared the custodian thought him mad. Mackintosh paid close attention to Ruskin's *The Stones of Venice*.

For all this, he decided that he wanted to create something new. He gave a talk in February 1893 to 'an audience chiefly composed of picture-painters'.[6] He began with 'the basis of certain ideas common to the architecture of many lands and religions, the purpose behind structure and form which may be called the true principles of architecture' but he was reading what he had copied in red ink (substituting 'true' later, in pencil, for 'esoteric') from the first paragraph of the preface of W. R. Lethaby's *Architecture, Mysticism and Myth* (1892). When Mackintosh read 'Old architecture lived because it had a purpose. Modern architecture, to be real, must not be a mere envelope without contents,' he had reached page seven. Just over half his talk is lifted from Lethaby. Towards the end Mackintosh slipped in: 'We must clothe modern ideas with modern dress — adorn our designs with living fancy. We shall have designs by living men for living men — of joy in nature, in grace of form, and gladness of colour.' This is a quotation from the architect J. D. Sedding,

again without acknowledgement. He very likely read these words in *The Builder* of October 1891 from a note by Lethaby on Sedding's death.

These statements, shamelessly plagiarised, were beliefs he strongly shared. His own words were forthright:

> How absurd it is to see modern churches, theatres, banks, museums, exchanges, municipal buildings, art galleries, etc, etc made in imitation of Greek temples. I am quite conscious of the dignity of Greek temples . . . but to be imported into this country and set up for such varied purposes, they must surely lose all their dignity. . . . There are many such buildings in Glasgow but to me they are as cold and lifeless as the cheek of a dead Chinaman.[7]

From Lethaby Mackintosh received encouragement, but little clue to the shape of a new architecture: 'What, then, will this art of the future be? The message will still be of nature and man, of order and beauty, but all will be sweetness, simplicity, freedom, confidence and light.' Nevertheless, many of these qualities, however vague, could be used to describe the School of Art.

In Lethaby's appreciation of Sedding, Mackintosh would also read words which were to become almost a slogan, in the sense of that word's Gaelic roots, a battle cry: 'There is hope in honest error; none in the icy perfections of the mere stylist.' In other words, better try something new and be wrong, than be a stylist churning out English Jacobean, Scholarly Gothic, Neo-Grec, Free Rustic Romanesque, Christian Free Byzantine, or even a Dutch Renaissance variation of Queen Anne. He used the slogan on a design for the invitation card for the School of Art Club meeting in November 1892. In 1901 he lettered it using his fully developed alphabet.

Under the title of Lethaby's book *Architecture, Mysticism and Myth* is a quotation from César Daly[8]: 'Are there symbols which may be called constant; proper to all races, all societies, and all countries?' Under that, in answer, are shown a circle and a square. Jungian psychology would agree for it recognises the circle as a symbol of the psyche,

11
Charles R. Mackintosh
INVITATION CARD TO GLASGOW SCHOOL
OF ART CLUB MEETING, 1892
Print, 12.6 × 21.5 cm
At the top is a treatment of 'There is hope . . .' Mackintosh also shows
symbolic thistles and two Sistine sybils

Glasgow School of Art Library

12
Charles R. Mackintosh
'THERE IS HOPE . . .' and
'DIE HOFFNUNG IST . . .', 1901
Print, 10 × 10.5 cm and 11.3 × 11.2 cm
The English version and the other (in shaky German) were reproduced
in Rudolf von Larisch's *Beispiele Kunstlerischer Schrift*, Vienna, 1902

Hunterian Art Gallery, University of Glasgow, Mackintosh Collection

13
W. R. Lethaby
TITLE PAGE AND FRONTISPIECE of
Architecture, Mysticism and Myth
Aberdeen City Libraries

14
NOTICE ABOVE THE ENTRANCE TO THE
SCHOOL
Painted wood, 46.4 × 46.4 cm

and the square as a symbol of the body and reality: the basic factors of life.[9] Perhaps it is too easy to leap to the conclusion that here is one of the germs of Mackintosh's own use of squares and circles. He designed a square sign, bordered with squares, for the School, which, in addition to its lettering, has four sets of squares each composed of four squares by four squares. Perhaps this sign says Glasgow School of Art, foursquare, i.e. solid and strong. He placed white, blue, and green tiles in permutations within a square in the walls of the staircases at each end of the School. He pierced the backs of the seats of the chairs for the Director's Room with sets of squares. He used them in doors and light fittings. Mackintosh invested the universal square with his inimitable art.

Circles bearing some of Mackintosh's own symbols are displayed along the front of the School. Lethaby quotes again from Daly: 'if we would have an architecture excite an interest, real and general, we must have a symbolism, immediately comprehensible by the great majority of spectators.' Mackintosh's symbols on these circles are perhaps not immediately comprehensible. They consist of a scarab, a ladybird, a bee, a bird (?) and an ant. Could the message read 'Here are [art] workers'?

15

TILES FROM THE STAIRCASES
Variations on 33 × 33 cm
These were part of the second phase of the
building

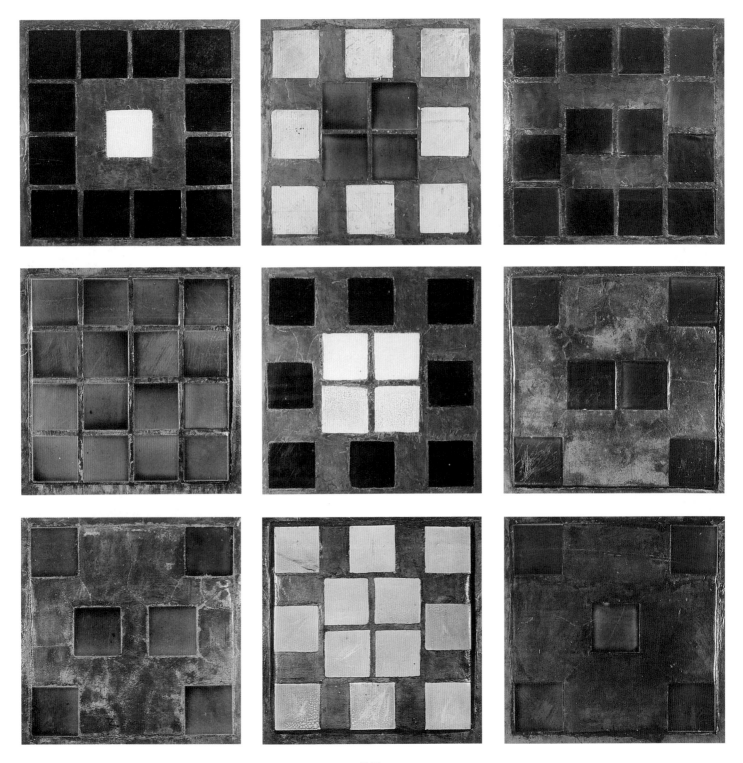

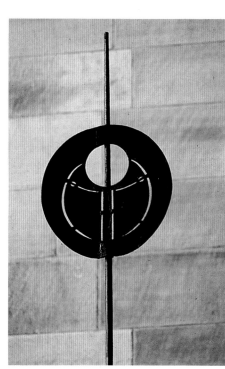

16
SYMBOLS ON THE RAILINGS
Wrought iron, each 64.3 cm high
l. to r. Scarab, Bird (?), Ant, Bee, Ladybird

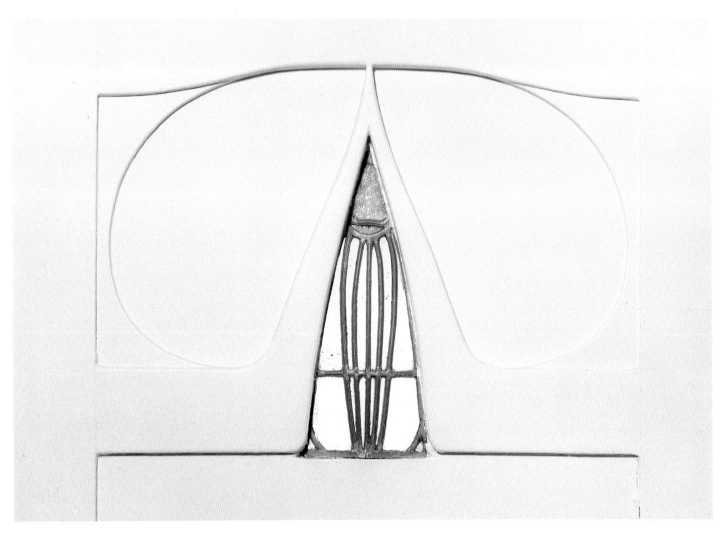

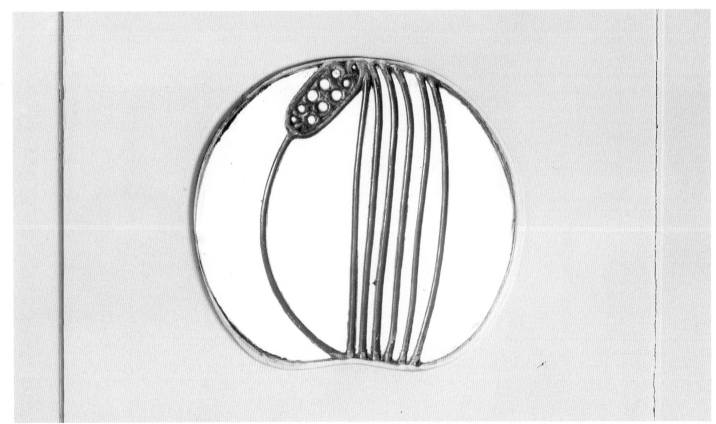

SYMBOLS IN DOORS
Stained-glass
Seed with roots from the Mackintosh Room,
31 cm high
Leaves and seed head from the Director's
Office, 19 cm high
Swift from a cupboard in the Director's Office,
19 cm high

The frontispiece of Lethaby's book shows the *Ziggu-rat of Belus at Babylon*. Perhaps this is Mackintosh's source for the stepped wall ends on the east staircase, or perhaps this form was created as a simple counterpoint to the steps themselves, or perhaps it is a version of the corbelling of Scottish vernacular architecture. It may be all, or some, or one, or none, of these strands of thought. Its highly practical use is discussed on p. 109.

Lethaby stated: 'Portals must have guardians.' The roundel above the School's entrance with which Mackintosh took so much care is surely such a guardian. Whether he intended them to act as guardians or not, Mackintosh placed little stained-glass insets in the doors of the School. These include butterflies and swifts, symbols of Mackintosh's own love of nature, and reminders of nature for people living in a huge smoky industrial city. In some cases the symbol is pre-cise: the seed head on the doors of the Director's Room is an apt symbol for learning.

Rosebuds appear in the doors of the superb set of stu-dios on the first floor and elsewhere. Mackintosh offers a clue

18
ROSEBUDS IN THE DOOR OF THE
REGISTRAR'S OFFICE
Stained-glass, 22 cm in length

19
ROSEBUDS
IN THE DOOR OF STUDIO 45   □■
Stained-glass, 73 × 45 cm

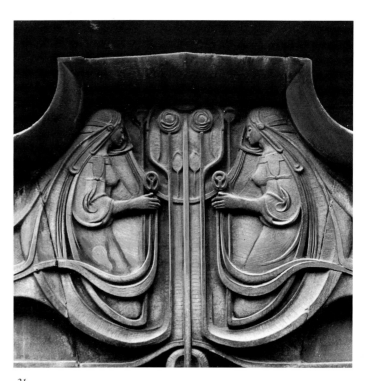

15

Let every artist strive to make his flower a beautiful living thing — something that will convince the world that there may be — there is are things more precious — more beautiful more lasting than life. But to do this you must offer real living — beautifully coloured flowers —— flowers that grow from but above the green leaf —— flowers that are not dead — are not dying — not artificial — real flowers springing from your own soul —— not even cut flowers —— You must offer the flowers of the art that is in you — the symbols of all that is noble — and beautiful —— and inspiring —— flowers that will often change a colourless cheerless life —— into an animated thoughtful thing.

How Beautiful the green leaf — how beautiful life often is — but think of the stupendous possibilities of the flower thus offered — of art. And it has been more towards art perhaps — more towards the flower I hope that I have tried to tempt your imagination tonight — tempted your imagination to the fact — that the craftsman of the future must be an artist — not what they too often are just now artistic failures

20

Charles R. Mackintosh
MANUSCRIPT FOR A LECTURE,
'Seemliness', 1902
Page 15 (of 17), 33 × 20.4 cm
Mackintosh writes of a leaf as a symbol for
life, and a flower as a symbol for art

Hunterian Art Gallery, University of Glasgow, Mackintosh Collection

21

RELIEF ABOVE THE SCHOOL ENTRANCE
Two figures, each holding a rose, act as
guardians to the School

to their meaning in a talk which he gave in 1902. The passage is so super-hyphenated that it could only be his. To paraphrase:

> Art is the flower. Life is the green leaf. Let every artist strive to make his flower a beautiful living thing. You must offer real, living, beautifully coloured flowers that grow above the green leaf. You must offer the flowers of the art that is in you, the symbols of all that is noble and beautiful and inspiring. How beautiful the green leaf. How beautiful life often is, but think of the stupendous possibilities of the flower thus offered — of art.[10]

The rosebud is, surely, Mackintosh's symbol for art. The two figures guarding the School's entrance each hold a rosebud and face a rosebush with its flowers standing clear above its leaves.

In his not altogether comprehensible book[11] Lethaby

22
FINIAL ON TOP OF EAST TOWER
Wrough iron, 224 × 76 cm
The two finials are not weathervanes but
versions of the city's coat-of-arms

propounded a 'cosmical symbolism'. A tree is both a symbol of the universe and, as an upright pole, a basic form of building construction. This immediately suggests the tree-poles along the front of the School standing above their metal leaves to carry Mackintosh's symbols of hard-working animals. The 'Tree of Life' became a trademark, almost, for Arts-and-Crafts-inspired architecture. It reached Vienna, and when, in the autumn of 1900, Mackintosh and his group exhibited in the Secession building, designed by his friend Joseph Olbrich,[12] he would see that it was capped with golden foliage and that its exterior walls were adorned with trees. The two iron trees which Mackintosh planted on the roof of the School have birds perched in them for they are versions of the city's coat of arms, although they could neatly combine both ideas.

The School's guardian roundel can also be seen as a Tree of Life. In showing a central column with two inward-facing figures, Mackintosh, consciously or not, was using a form with ancient roots.[13] Mackintosh also set, in glass, into doors on the ground floor the outline of a tree. Its trunk is clearly shown, but in the foliage the face of a woman emerges. A tight rosebud lies half-way between her head and feet. This is more likely to be an unconscious use of symbolism by Mackintosh in relation to Margaret Macdonald his future wife. Mackintosh developed the rosebud motif and, like his square, he made a version of it his own. The rosebud was also taken up by others in Glasgow. If a 'Tree of Life' is the symbol of the English (not British) Arts and Crafts movement, then the rosebud is the same for the Glasgow (not Scottish) movement. It is a highly charged, sensuous symbol. The difference between the work of these two groups was perceptively noted by the German writer Hermann Muthe-

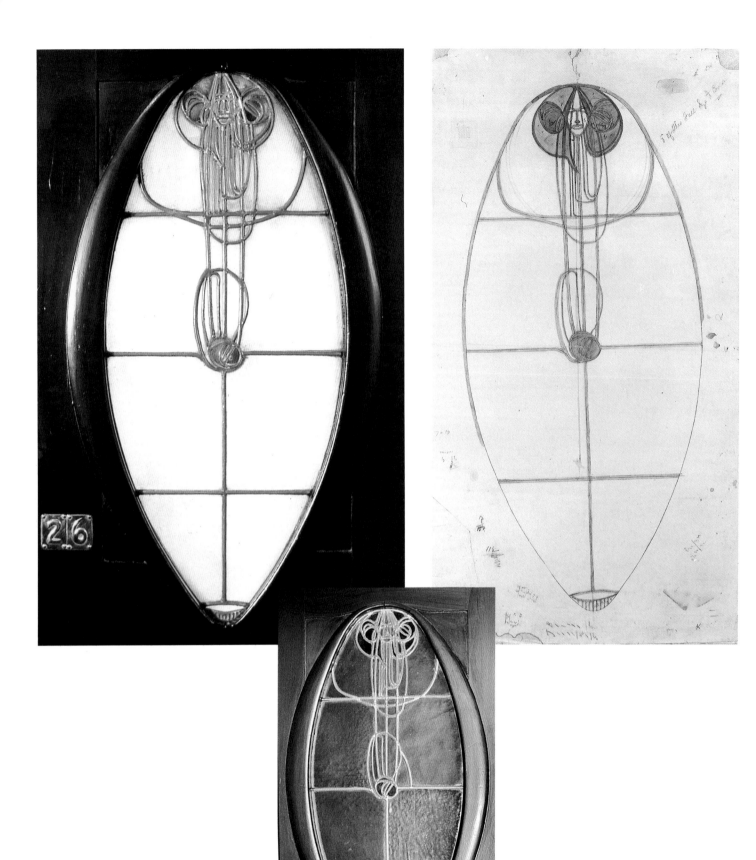

23

▪▫ TREE/WOMAN IN GROUND-FLOOR DOORS
Stained-glass, height 90 cm
These glass panels also work when lit from
the front
Door of Studio 26
Door of Studio 25

24

Charles R. Mackintosh
▫▪ DESIGN FOR LEADED GLASS INSET IN
SCHOOL DOORS, c. 1899
Pencil and watercolour, 103.5 × 55.45 cm
Hunterian Art Gallery, University of Glasgow,
Mackintosh Collection

sius who suggested that the imagination was suppressed in English work, while in Glasgow it was imagination which drove the work.[14]

It was in architectural magazines, such as *The Builder,* that Mackintosh saw the work of architects who inspired him. In his talk in 1893 he named them: R. Norman Shaw; John Francis Bentley; John Belcher; George Frederick Bodley; Leonard A. Stokes; and John Dando Sedding. They were, he said 'quite as great if not greater artists than the best living painters, men who more and more are freeing themselves from correct antiquarian detail and who go straight to nature'. To this list he might have added C. F. A. Voysey and J. M. MacLaren.

Mackintosh also knew about the art of Japan. Like any young up-to-the-minute student he had had Japanese prints on the wall of his room. Prints were easily available in Glasgow. The School's library has now, and probably had then, Bing's beautiful periodical *Artistic Japan.* The top studio in the School's western tower has a Japanese-like beam construction. The symbols on the railings were designed by someone who knew *Mon,* family crests. These are specific examples, though often it is more one of mood. An occasional, exotic, whiff of Japan pervades the School.[15]

Mackintosh's mind must have been full of these diverse ideas while creating the School of Art. David M. Walker, who, like Howarth, Macleod, and Kimura,[16] has carefully sought out Mackintosh's sources, properly reminds us:

> no designer can shake off subconscious memory, training and custom altogether . . . Even where antecedents can be found or suggested, it would be wrong to insist on them too strongly. Motifs are transformed both in detail and setting in a remarkably original way. There is no precedent for the design [of the School] as a whole.[17]

On 25 May 1898 the foundation stone was laid. Inside it was a glass jar containing a history of the School lettered by a student, Jessie M. King, and signed by the representatives of the many bodies present. After a speech by the Lord Provost the stone was lowered between two large windows on the first floor. It was said to be in full view of Renfrew Street although it

can neither be seen nor located today. Sir Renny Watson did the official deed, but as he was given a solid silver trowel, the Lord Provost an ebony mallet mounted in silver, and Fleming a silver plummet, perhaps all three were involved. After hearty cheers the party returned to the Corporation Galleries where they toasted the School with wine and cake. At least that is according to one report. A bill for this junket discloses that they drank champagne (Heidsieck '92), claret and sherry, and ate lobster, crab, *foie gras,* and chicken, followed by strawberries, pineapples and grapes. The bill came to £66 — about £2800 in present-day terms!

Mr FRANCIS H. NEWBERY,
Head Master,— Glasgow School of Art.

26
Artist unknown
MR FRANCIS H. NEWBERY, 1898
Published in *The Bailie*, 25 May 1898, p. 5,
to coincide with the laying of the School's
foundation stone. 'An able organiser, and well
fitted to hold his own part in all discussions'
Glasgow Room, Mitchell Library

27
Photographer unknown
JOHN KEPPIE, n d
From *Glasgow Institute of Architects Album*,
vol 2, pl. 19
Glasgow School of Art Library

Nowhere in these proceedings was Mackintosh's name mentioned. It was John Keppie who sat on the platform and who was reported in the *Glasgow Herald* as the architect.[18] It was Keppie who was to conduct the business with the School, to show the Governors round the site. A letter from Mackintosh to Muthesius written on 11 May, two weeks before these celebrations took place, explains the situation:

> You must understand that for the time being I am under a cloud — as it were — although the building in Mitchell Street[19] here was designed by me the architects are or were Messrs Honeyman & Keppie — who employ me as *assistant*. So if you reproduce any photographs of the building you must give the architects' name — not mine. You will see that is very unfortunate for me, but I hope when brighter days come, I shall be able to work for myself entirely and claim my work as mine.[20]

Mackintosh, now thirty, was six years younger than Keppie, but light years ahead of him as a creative architect. It makes Mackintosh's achievement all the more astonishing when one realises what little experience he had had.

It poured on the afternoon of Wednesday 20 December 1899 when Newbery's younger daughter Mary presented, on a white cushion, the long key to Sir James King to open the new School. Once inside, there were nine speeches, including one by Keppie. That evening past and present students attended two concerts and danced until 2 a.m. The women wore satin, brocade, velvet and silk in dominant colours of green, pink, black, white and heliotrope. These colours were seen against the woodwork of the School which was painted, according to the *Evening Times*, 'an artistic shade of green'. It would be strangely unfamiliar to anyone used to the School's present dark woodwork. A certain Miss Macdonald was noted whose 'auburn hair was well

28
STUDIO 45
A cluttered and paint-spattered studio of the
1980s

29
BALCONY, STUDIO 45
Several studios have had balconies inserted
to cope with the growing numbers of students

set off with her fawn dress'.[21] Here is the future Mrs Mackintosh wearing her liberated Aesthetic dress.

The *Evening Times*, next day, assessed the building perceptively: 'Externally it is as everyone, with an appreciation of artistic simplicity and fine design, is bound to confess a structure which will long remain as a monument to the strong originality and artistic conception of the Glasgow designers. The opinions were . . . all expressive of admiration.' *Building Industries* on 16 January 1900 bemoaned 'the running up of a house of correction, or poorhouse', though it conceded that 'the originality is unquestionable.' While the accusation has been made that Mackintosh's domestic interiors are too perfect for comfort, this can not be said of the School, where paint continues to fly, turpentine to spill, and mess as well as art is created. The building works superbly.

The satisfaction of erecting even half the building must have been tempered when in September 1901 the Governors learned that the costs had been exceeded by more than a third. It is clear that Mackintosh regarded plans as an indication of intention rather than a solution to problems. In this overspending Keppie must take a share for he was clearly the responsible partner in the firm. It would seem likely that here is a source of their reported enmity in addition to their differences of opinion about new architecture. The Governors appealed to the Scottish Education Department, the Bellahouston Bequest Fund and to Glasgow Corporation all of which gave further substantial grants, but it was to be February, four years later, before this overspending was finally cleared. Meanwhile, the first half of the School became as cramped as its old quarters in Rose Street. There was no lecture theatre. The Museum was not properly in use,

for half contained the Library and the other half was used for drawing from the antique.

In January 1906 Newbery began the completion of the building. Yet again the School began to raise money. Through Fleming's indefatigable skill £13,275 (£557,000) was amassed. Templeton's contributed £500, double their first donation. Again Fleming contributed handsomely: this time £200. The sum of £100 each was given by the publishers Blackie, the Scottish Co-operative Wholesale Society,

and Honeyman, Keppie & Mackintosh. The tea-room tycoon, Miss Cranston, gave £20. The venerable Glasgow Boy W. Y. Macgregor sent £10, and the staff and students made collections, the former raising £36, the latter £39. This time the Scottish Education Department added £15,000, plus a later contribution.

In retrospect we have to be thankful that there was *not* enough money to build the entire School first time. For, between the completion of the first part, in December 1899,

34
Muirhead Bone
□ ■ BUILDING THE SCHOOL OF ART,
RENFREW STREET, 1908
Drawing 17.7 × 13.2 cm
From *Glasgow: Fifty Drawings,* Maclehose,
1911, plate 41
Glasgow School of Art Library

33
Tom Maxwell
GLASGOW SCHOOL OF ART. Sketch of the
Proposed Extension, 1907
The view, from the *Glasgow Herald,* 26 June
1907, shows that three trees, like those at the
east end, were also to be planted at the west
end. The attic studios are not shown
although it is mentioned that these were
intended for professors, advanced students
and artists visiting the city
Glasgow Room, Mitchell Library

and February 1907, when Honeyman, Keppie & Mackintosh, were formally appointed architects, Mackintosh had created Windyhill, The Hill House, Scotland Street School, Tearooms for Miss Cranston, designs for the 1901 Glasgow Exhibition and exhibitions in Turin and Vienna. Yet during that time he was clearly oppressed by the weight of opinion against him. Another letter to Muthesius, this time on 4 September 1902, reveals the extent of this opposition: 'Yes, we know only too well how many people are against us, but I am very sorry to hear that anyone condemns you for writing about our work.'[22] But Mackintosh had strength as this description of him in 1903 bears out: '. . . tall, dressed all in black, with long dark hair parted in the middle . . . the general appearance is of a clean-shaven American clergyman who is still pulsing with the emotion and travail of his last metaphysical discourse but has succeeded, by powers of restraint, in preserving an impassivity and an unnatural silence.'[23] With the maturity he had gained he re-designed completely the west façade of the School, creating the breathtaking and now famous Library tower.

When the Building Committee (appointed in September 1906 under Patrick S. Dunn) pressed Mackintosh for plans in March 1907, he replied, 'We think it undesirable to commit ourselves to any elevational treatment until the general scheme of internal arrangement is approved.' The plans went to the Building Committee in April when they were approved. This was confirmed by the Governors in June. They were sent to the Measurers (i.e. Quantity Surveyors) and the scheme was finally cleared by the Governors in August.

On 26 June 1907 there appeared in the *Glasgow Herald* a sketch of the proposed extension to the School. The accompanying text made it clear that the work was being carried out under the supervision of Mackintosh (now a partner in the firm). There was mention of sculpture between the library windows to represent art, architecture, sculpture, and music. Elsewhere, a note by Mackintosh suggests that the subjects would be Cellini, Palladio and St Francis, but the £1000 set aside for carving on the second stage of the building was held back by the Committee.

It is understandable that the Governors should wish to exercise tight control over finance. They issued instructions to contractors that they could deviate from the agreed plan only if such alterations had been approved in writing by the

41

35
Tom Maxwell
ARCHITECTURE, 1909
Mackintosh, no doubt in characteristic pose
nursing his pipe, appeared in 'Prominent
Profiles', *Evening Times,* 15 Dec. 1909, the
day the completed School was opened
Glasgow Room, Mitchell Library

36
Alexander McGibbon
GLASGOW SCHOOL OF ART, 1925
From the School Calendar, 1934-5, p. 5. The
building at last complete. Inexplicably,
McGibbon, now Professor of Architectural
Design, shows all the large studio windows
four panes of glass wide   *Glasgow School of Art Library*

Committee. This was not adhered to, so, on 5 February 1908 a letter was sent from the Convenor:

> Referring to my informal conversation with your Mr Keppie in the Art Club today it is right that the views of the Governors should be put before you formally. Six of the Governors inspected the newly erected sub-basement Porch and Entrance in Scott Street and were surprised to find that the work was carried out in an extravagant manner and not in accordance with the plans and estimate which were submitted and signed. I beg to intimate that we must decline all liability for any increase of cost.

Mackintosh's reply that he would make savings elsewhere to cover these costs was not accepted. The Governors next asked for a monthly report on progress. This was done, so it is easy to chart the progress of the new building which included the service stair for the east end, and the rise of the west tower to contain the long-awaited Lecture Theatre and Library. Between October and November 1908 a steam crane puffed busily as it hauled up materials.

In February 1909 there was a proposal to remove the balcony shown running across the windows in the Library. Mackintosh replied that it would upset the proportion and design of the room and that it would increase the cost to do

37
WALL CLOCK
Wood, 50.2 × 51.4 cm
There are two sizes of clocks. The smaller
measures 41.9 cm square

so. The balcony remained. In May the builder finished his contract. In September the joiners, painters and electricians were finishing the last details.

In December the building was formally opened. New-bery excelled himself with a series of exhibitions and celebrations over several days. The official proceedings took place at 2.30 on Wednesday 15 December. There was a reception in the Museum which was hung with work by former students including Lavery, Henry, and Pringle. This time Mackintosh was clearly identified as the creator of the building; he even spoke. He presented a casket which he had designed, and Peter Wylie Davidson had made, to (now) Sir James Fleming. The party descended to the ground floor where Sir James threw aside the curtain which divided the old from the new. That evening at another reception a symbolic masque written by Newbery, *The Birth and Growth of Art*, was performed twice by a huge number of students in the Architecture School in the north-west corner of the new building. The climax is reached when A Male Student declaims:

> *How Art, with loving care, this shrine of Hers*
> *Doth place as goodly gift in Glasgow's hands*

to which A Female Student adds, with a less than Shakespearian ring:

> *Fall! Good St Mungo's Blessings on this School*
> *Its work make prosper, and its Fame let spread!*

The Governors' report for the session 1908-9 described the new School thus:

> The Glasgow School of Art is now a completed structure. On the first floor the façade windows have been supplemented by roof lights, so that the volume of light admitted is the greatest possible. A room with entrance from Dalhousie Street has been provided for the use of students of the living animal.[24] The Library . . . is well lighted by those long windows that make a striking feature of the west elevation . . . and quietness and seclusion are secured. The building is lighted throughout with electricity and electrically controlled clocks have

39

Francis Newbery

THE BUILDING COMMITTEE OF THE
GLASGOW SCHOOL OF ART, 1913-14

Oil, 133 × 171 cm

Standing: Charles R. Mackintosh FRIBA;
D. Barclay FRIBA; J. M. Munro FRIBA;
H. Reid DL; Dr J. J. Burnet RSA, FRIBA;
J. M. Groundwater (Secretary).
Sitting: Col R. J. Bennett VD;
Sir Francis Powell LL D, PRSW;
Patrick S. Dunn (Chairman);
Councillor J. Mollison MINA;
Sir W. Bilsland Bart LL D, DL;
John Henderson MA; Sir James Fleming
(Chairman of the Board); Francis Newbery

Glasgow School of Art

BUILDING COMMITTEE OF THE GLASGOW SCHOOL OF ART

been provided throughout the building. The School is warmed and ventilated throughout upon the Plenum system. The Life Rooms are further heated by low-pressure steam coils. The Architects are Messrs Honeyman, Keppie & Mackintosh.

In their Annual Report for the session 1909-10, the Governors gave their official verdict. They were 'not aware of any city that possesses a more complete edifice devoted to Art Education, nor one better adapted to its purpose'. Even more satisfying to them, perhaps, was that by December 1910 the costs of the building had been entirely covered.

To commemorate their successful work Newbery painted a group portrait of the Building Committee. He showed it at the (now) Royal Glasgow Institute of the Fine Arts exhibition, then presented it to the School. It was formally accepted on 18 May 1914. Sometime before the presentation he added to the painting the figure of the School's architect. Newbery's portrait of Mackintosh had been a study for this figure. To accommodate Mackintosh a strip of canvas had had to be added to the side. If Mackintosh looks a little uncomfortable it may be because of his very late arrival. It may also reflect something of the strained relations between the Committee and its servant. This painting now hangs in the Board Room — the very room it depicts — where the furniture, the clock, the ink-well, all remain. In the painting sits a hunched Fleming. He had attended the presentation of the portrait but died six days later. On the right sits Newbery. On the left stands Mackintosh. Could Fleming, Newbery, or even Mackintosh have ever dreamt what, one day, might be said about their School? 'One of the great works of Arts and Crafts genius of the turn of the century'[25]; 'the Free Style soaring to heights it never quite reached elsewhere ... the Free Style's masterpiece'[26]; 'one of the greatest monuments of modern architecture in Europe.'[27] Beyond Mackintosh's wildest dreams would be the claim that the School is now 'as necessary a building to visit and study as the Parthenon or Chartres were for earlier generations.'[28]

Would Mackintosh have believed that he 'single-handed . . . invented in one way or another almost the whole vocabulary of the modern movement',[29] that he is not only 'one of the last and one of the greatest of the Victorians'[30], but also 'an important forerunner of the functional architecture of the post-Second World War period'?[31]

The School, atop its drumlin in Garnethill, where once could be heard 'the sounds of the river: sirens and steam-whistles on foggy days, the clangour of the shipyards when the wind was set from there'[32], 'is a building that we should cherish intently. It so clearly exemplifies all that is best in the revolt against historicism and clutter. It is still a powerful modern building, a powerful Scottish building and one that proclaims something of the universal essence of architecture.'[33] What is to be heard, most clearly above all, in its corridors and staircases, its rooms and its studios, is the strong, clear, passionate voice of its creator.

40
Robin Ward
GLASGOW SCHOOL OF ART, 1976
From Robin Ward *Some City Glasgow*,
Richard Drew, 1982, p. 112·3
The motor car now besieges the School;
students wear flared trousers

Glasgow School of Art Library

NOTES

1   This centralised course is laid out in great detail in the Department of Science and Art's annual directories.

2   Smith's prize-winning *Design for a City Club* is illustrated in *The British Architect*, 19 Dec. 1884, between pp. 298 and 299. In 1887 Smith (who lived in Coatbridge) was awarded a bonus because of the good results in his classes. He resigned in June 1895.

3   Illustrated in *The British Architect*, 10 June 1892, p. 432.

4   I am grateful to the Institute of Chartered Accountants of Scotland for this information.

5   'Scotch Baronial Architecture', F(c). Quoted by permission of the Hunterian Art Gallery, University of Glasgow, Mackintosh Collection.

6   'Paper on Architecture' F(h). Quoted by permission of the Hunterian Art Gallery.

7   *ibid.*

8   César Daly (1810-93), a French architect and writer, who sought the incontestable principles of architecture and wished that symbolism be considered as part of architectural education. He advocated an institute of advanced study. Awarded the RIBA Gold Medal in 1892. For a recent plea see the writings of Charles Jencks e.g. *Towards a Symbolic Architecture*, Academy Editions, 1985.

9   Aniela Jaffé, 'Symbolism in the Visual Arts', in Carl Jung (ed.), *Man and his Symbols*, Picador, 1978, p. 285.

10   'Seemliness', F(e). Quoted by permission of the Hunterian Art Gallery.

11   Lethaby re-wrote it as *Architecture, Nature and Magic* in a series of articles for *The Builder* in 1928. It was published as a book by Duckworth in 1956. *Architecture, Mysticism, and Myth* has been reprinted, with an introduction by Godfrey Rubens, by the Architectural Press, in 1975 and 1976.

12   Its foundation stone was laid on 28 April 1898 a few weeks before that of the School's.

13   For example, the Lion Gate at Mycenae where the carving of two animals facing a central pillar guards the entrance to the Citadel and Palace. Illustrated in Leonard Cottrell, *The Lion Gate*, Evans Brothers, 1963, Frontispiece.

14   See the translation of Muthesius's book (with an introduction by Dennis Sharp) *The English House*, Crosby, Lockwood, Staples, London, 1979, p. 51.

15   Dr Hiroaki Kimura, 'Japanese Influences, 1900', and William Buchanan, 'Willows East and West', both in the Catalogue *Charles Rennie Mackintosh*, Japan Art and Culture Association, Tokyo, 1985.

16   Thomas Howarth, *Charles Rennie Mackintosh and the Modern Movement*, Routledge & Kegan Paul, London, 1952 and 1977; Robert Macleod, *Charles Rennie Mackintosh*, Country Life, 1968 and revised as *Charles Rennie Mackintosh: Architect and Artist*, Collins, 1983; David M. Walker 'The Early Work of Mackintosh', in Nikolaus Pevsner & J. M. Richards (eds.), *The Anti-Rationalists*, Architectural Press, London, 1973; Hiroaki Kimura, *Charles Rennie Mackintosh*, Process Architecture, Tokyo, 1984.

17   David M. Walker, 'The Early Work of Charles Rennie Mackintosh', in Nikolaus Pevsner & J. M. Richards (eds.), *The Anti-Rationalists*, Architectural Press, 1973, pp. 116 and 129.

18   This idea persisted. George Eyre-Todd in *Who's Who in Glasgow in 1909*, Gowans & Gray, London, 1909 states that Keppie built the School.

19   *Glasgow Herald* extension.

20   I am grateful to Pamela Robertson, Curator, Hunterian Art Gallery, University of Glasgow, Mackintosh Collection, for showing me this letter and to Eckart Muthesius for permission to quote from it.

21   Scotia, 'Scottish Society Notes', *Madame*, 6 Jan. 1900, p. 15.

22   Illustrated in *Hermann Muthesius 1861-1927*, Catalogue, Architectural Association, 1979, p. 31.

23   B. E. Kalas, *De la Tamise à la Sprée*, Michaud, Rheims, 1905.

24   This is at the east end. Animals, including an elephant, were brought from Hengler's Circus round the corner in Sauchiehall Street. One day, a camel bumped its hump on the door and ran amok.

25   Peter Davey, *Arts and Crafts Architecture*, Architectural Press, 1980, p. 136.

26   Alastair Service, *Edwardian Architecture*, Thames & Hudson, 1977, p. 58.

27   Patrick Nuttgens, *Understanding Modern Architecture*, Unwin Hyman, 1988, p. 49.

28   Nuttgens, *ibid.*, p. 56.

29   Ian Nairn, 'Glasgow and Cumbernauld New Town', *The Listener*, 10 Nov. 1960, p. 831.

30   Robert Macleod, *Charles Rennie Mackintosh*, Country Life Books, 1968, p. 156.

31   Mario Amaya, *Art Nouveau*, Dutton Vista, 1966, p. 54.

32   Catherine Carswell, *Lying Awake: An Unfinished Autobiography*, Secker & Warburg, 1950, p. 20.

33   Denys Lasdun, 'Charles Rennie Mackintosh: A Personal View', in Patrick Nuttgens (ed.), *Mackintosh and his Contemporaries: in Europe and America*, John Murray, London, 1988, p. 153.

A MODERN ENIGMA
A PARADOX OF REDUCTION AND ENRICHMENT

ANDREW MACMILLAN

THE Glasgow School of Art is not only the masterwork of its creator, Charles Rennie Mackintosh, and the seminal British building of its decade, 1897-1907, but is the first great monument of modern architecture, the first building that is, to derive its authority from its own intrinsic nature rather than from its employment of any stylistic or historical canon.

That it was built in Glasgow in the decade spanning the turn of the century may seem surprising today, but the Glasgow of that time was a vital city, the industrial powerhouse of a world-wide empire. Vigorous and enterprising in its industry and commerce, it was equally adventurous in its artistic activities. This upsurge of artistic energy in turn-of-the-century Glasgow related in many ways to a world-wide situation and useful parallels can be drawn with the emergence of Wright and the Prairie School in Chicago, Gaudí and Catalan Modernismo in Barcelona, and Horta and Guimard and art nouveau in Brussels and Paris; all serving the same 'arriviste' clientele who, deriving enormous, personal wealth from expanding trade and industry, sought new artistic expression to match or bolster their own distinctive way of living rather as had the rich Florentine merchants of the Renaissance.

That Glasgow was in the forefront of this new expression, therefore, was an accurate reflection of its situation in the burgeoning international economy of the times and in 1896 its new School of Art was conceived in that stimulating milieu. Envisaged as a place to educate artists, architects and designers for their role in the new industrial society, it was part of a nationwide art school system with a common curriculum and common aims. Yet in the end it was different, revolutionary even.

In Glasgow the pervasive presence of industry, of shipbuilding and heavy engineering may well have engendered a more commonplace acceptance of state-of-the-art technology and the use of machinery with less stress, perhaps, laid on the precious exercise of traditional craft. This innovatory environment coupled with the acknowledged dynamism of the new Head of the School, Francis Newbery, may well have been critical in providing the necessary, fertile seedbed for a young talent and a new architecture to flourish.

Today, some ninety years after its conception and long after the demise of art nouveau and the English Free Style, Mackintosh's School of Art continues to intrigue and inspire and has become a Mecca for architectural pilgrims. That not only historians but major practising architects continue to come to the School to see it for themselves is perhaps surprising. To understand why, it is useful to perceive the building as it is now, or even as it might have seemed when it first appeared, and also to understand that at the time it was first conceived the emerging Modern Movement stood poised at a choice of ways forward.

Now, the School can be seen clearly as belonging firmly in the new architecture, yet displaying unselfconsciously an awareness of its architectural heritage, drawing its authority from Mackintosh's informed comprehension of the meaning of historical building forms, both architectural and perhaps more importantly for the future at that time, vernacular. His surviving sketchbooks make clear the focus of his studies. His buildings display the fruits and nowhere more clearly than in the School. Here, over ten formative years of building, can be seen the development of his talent from the use, as a young man, of relatively direct derivations of Scottish picturesque forms at the south-east end, to the mature, sophisticated intellectual and artistic invention of the south and west gables of the later Library wing.

Also very clear in the younger Mackintosh's first stage design is the debt he owed to C. F. A. Voysey, some ten years his senior and then a leading member of the English Free School. But how quickly Mackintosh's ambition and understanding can be seen to outstrip that of his mentor, and even at the beginning his completed 1897-9 wing demonstrated a scale and a clarity of idea which Voysey never achieved, substantially composed though it was, of borrowings from his work.[1]

A major point of departure from the aims of the English movement was Mackintosh's willingness to absorb and utilise the new technologies of the time: central heating,

41
Brian & Shere
GLASGOW SCHOOL OF ART, c. 1955
Photograph
This view, taken one summer morning
judging by the shadows cast by the window
brackets, no longer exists. It is now cluttered
with cars, street signs, and lamp posts
Glasgow School of Art Library

42
EAST FAÇADE □■□

43
WEST FAÇADE □□■

electric light, machine-finished timber, plate glass, etc., something which today can be seen to connect Mackintosh to the mainstream of modern architecture as it was so soon to develop and link him indirectly with Wright in Chicago. The publication in 1910 of the famous Wasmuth Portfolio of Frank Lloyd Wright's work in Chicago had the same revolutionary quality as the House for an Art Lover had in 1901, and seemed a confirmation of the promise of abstraction hinted at in Mackintosh's work. Like him, too, Wright revealed the influence of Japan.

Of particular interest now is the decorative manner in which Mackintosh integrated these technologies into the overall design of the School, the timber ducts, square-gridded metal grilles, electric conduiting and junction boxes, all exploited effortlessly in a tectonic totality. It is small wonder that for his European contemporaries, the striking black and white photographs by Annan and Lemere of the School interiors were confirmation that a new age of architectural honesty had dawned, that a meaningful new architecture was possible.[2]

At the time too, for those who saw them, his experiments with the façade treatments were equally radical and revealing. A different elevational rationale was explored on each and every façade of the building; a-historical yet referential, these elevational treatments derived their power from the successful architectural and functional resolution of the internal and external forces acting simultaneously at the façade. They bore witness, too, to Mackintosh's comprehension of the intrinsic meaning of vernacular building as deriving from the interaction of, and response to, the needs of the occupants, and the constructional discipline imposed by the actual process of building.

This revelation was Mackintosh's major contribution to mainstream modern architecture and undoubtedly guided its direction in central Europe towards the functionalism which developed in the 1920s and 1930s. That architecture could be poetic yet draw its strength and its rationale from the process of building, was Mackintosh's main message, one particularly understood by his contemporaries in

Vienna. That it need not depend on handcraft was another. The School of Art is a demonstration of how the use of machine finishes could be subsumed in the aesthetics of the building.

Visible here, too, as in all of Mackintosh's major works, was the influence of Japanese architecture, now recognised as significant to the development of modern architecture as was African art to Cubism. Clearly displayed in the School (and also noticeable in the Annan photographs of Mackintosh's own house), it can be seen directly borrowed in the decorative roundels of the front railings and indirectly in the whole attitude to the use and exploitation of material demonstrated in the School, as, for example, in the grained surfaces and shaped mouldings of the ubiquitous internal timber panelling and doors.

Thus from a fortuitous conjunction of industrial Glasgow's direct relationship with contemporary Japan, particularly through shipbuilding, and the revelations of contemporary English architecture and art in the newly published *The Studio* magazine, came necessary, catalytic elements for the emergence in Mackintosh's work of a process-oriented approach to the creation of a new non-historic (in a Western sense) architecture. Through Newbery, too, with his invited exhibition of the work of the English Arts and Crafts Exhibition Society and invitations to luminaries such as William Morris to come and speak in Glasgow, Mackintosh would have had first-hand experience of the aims and artefacts of that movement.

The Japanese experience, once understood, clarified the meaning of the pioneering contribution of the earlier English House Movement in programmatic and tectonic[3] terms and guided Mackintosh, and those of his contemporaries with eyes to see, out of the historicist cul-de-sac within which their expressed desire for a new 'national' architecture might have entrapped them for ever. Curiously, once again, today for architects this cosy but dangerous nationalist diversion has reappeared, and current interest in Mackintosh and the School reflects a need to reconsider basic principles, at an intellectual level, rather than drift into the sort of facile, formalist borrowing only too clearly evidenced in the work of some 'contemporary' architects, e.g. Quinlan Terry in Britain, Leon Krier in Europe and Alan Greenberg in the United States.

In trying to see the School as it must have seemed when it was first built at the threshold of the present century, surely it was clear even then that here was a modern structure, revolutionary yet monumental, a public building, simple but with an impressive scale and presence. Displaying a variety of architectural 'events', it made little or no reference to historical architecture as it was then understood, in the sense of the 'styles', an inherited vocabulary of symbolic forms. Liberated from the need for stylistic conformity and constraint, this building seemed able to assert its inner nature, yet reveal in the process a strong structural discipline, which saved it from eccentricity or artistic licence.

In his *Das englische Haus* of 1904, Muthesius commented thus on Mackintosh's contributions:

> Mackintosh with his strong architectonic sense sees to it that proper architectonic values are maintained . . . and his ground plans are models of practicality and are comfortable and convenient.

An anonymous contributor to *The Studio* of 15 February 1900 had this more particular observation to offer:

> The building has been designed to meet the requirements of the school, and in no instance has a regard for appearance been allowed to interfere with these special requirements. Embellishments have been carefully concentrated, and gain in value from their juxtaposition to plain surfaces. The great windows to the north are a conspicuous feature in the elevations, and the projecting roof gives sufficient light and shade to emphasise the scale. All details have been carefully worked out, and the building possesses a unique character due in some measure to requirements and situation, but in the highest degree to the treatment of the subject by the architect.

Today, creative architects see present in the School possibilities and options for modernism that were never taken up and find confirmation both of the 'rightness' of their 'modern' approach, and of their urgent wish to enrich the modernist vocabulary. Recognising public disillusionment with the state of Western cities, with the facile repetition everywhere of system building and the mindless destruction of historic structured communities for administrative convenience or ruthless private gain, they are seriously reassessing the ideas of the Modern Movement and re-examining its values against those of the architecture it superseded. This present state of architectural public debate has been continuing since the 1970s. Its fruits are now beginning to appear in our schools and in our current magazines.

The School offers example in its richness and its manifest uniqueness. A type, the Art School, yet specific, the Glasgow School of Art, it is a singular edifice built in a specific city, at a moment in time. It uncannily approaches Tony Vidler's definition of the third typology as 'emptied of specific social content from any particular time, speaking only of its own formal conditions'[4]. These latter, of course, can now be seen to extend beyond the programmatic.

Mackintosh's most singular characteristic for architects and designers, now as then, is his astonishing ability to reshape everyday objects and transform them into iconic images of great potency. His objects, be they buildings or furniture, are unique and memorable with a powerful, physical presence lacking in the artefacts of the Heroic Modern, which in many ways sought anonymity rather than individuality, revelling in the inevitability of serial repetition rather than in exploring the process of industrialisation towards variety and choice. The authority with which Mackintosh's furniture occupies and dominates its immediate spatial domain remains a powerful enigma even today, a challenge that Moderns from Aldo Van Eyck to Richard Meier have found irresistible. The paradox is that side by side with his sober, conscientious examination of the nature of building evidenced in the sketchbooks, he exercised as an architect and an artist a poetic sensibility, personal, inventive, and above

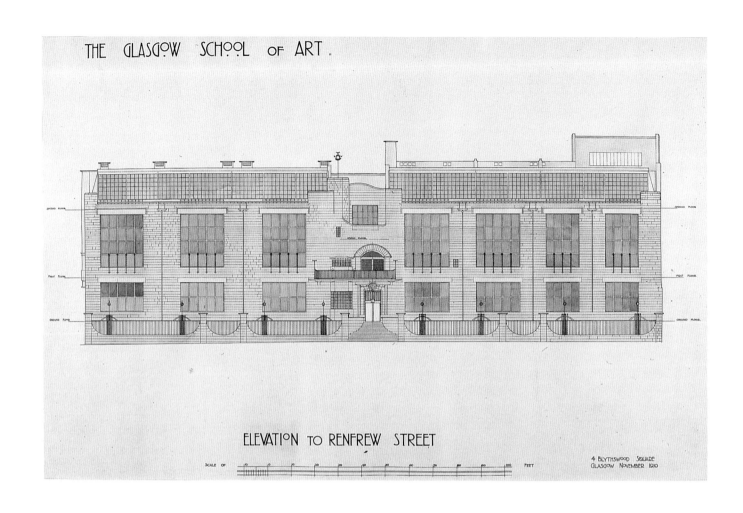

THE GLASGOW SCHOOL OF ART.

ELEVATION TO RENFREW STREET

SCALE OF ⊢⊢⊢⊢⊢⊢⊢ FEET

4 BLYTHSWOOD SQUARE
GLASGOW NOVEMBER 1910

46
Charles R. Mackintosh
THREE DRAWINGS FROM A SET OF TEN,
November 1910
These were made at 4 Blythswood Square
eleven months after the opening of the
building. See also nos 52, 82
Glasgow School of Art

■□ *a* ELEVATION TO RENFREW STREET
□□ (i.e. North Elevation)
Ink and watercolour, 57.5 × 91 cm

□□ *b* ELEVATION TO SCOTT STREET,
■■ ELEVATION TO DALHOUSIE STREET
(i.e. West and East Elevations)
Pencil, ink and watercolour, 59 × 85 cm

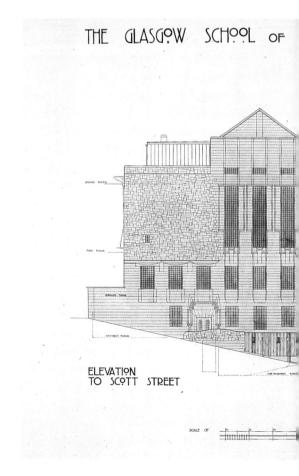

THE GLASGOW SCHOOL OF

ELEVATION
TO SCOTT STREET

SCALE OF

THE GLASGOW SCHOOL OF ART.

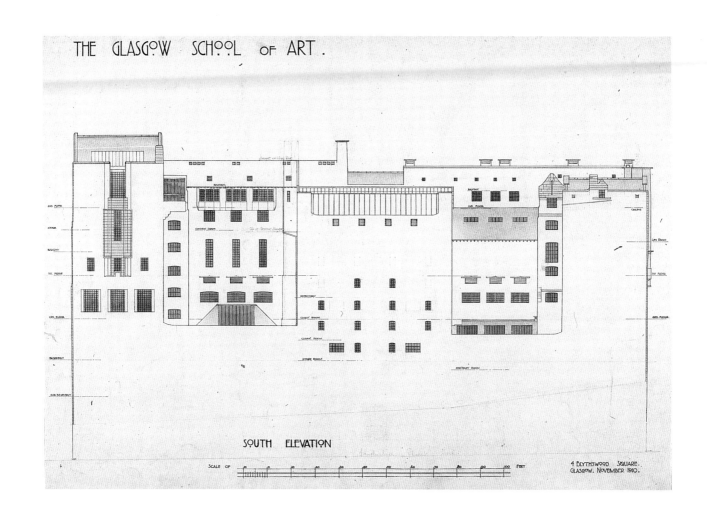

SOUTH ELEVATION

SCALE OF   FEET

4 BLYTHSWOOD SQUARE.
GLASGOW. NOVEMBER 1910.

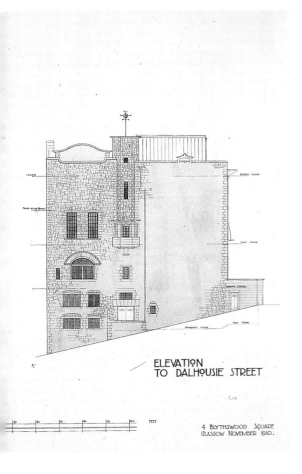

ELEVATION
TO DALHOUSIE STREET

FEET

4 BLYTHSWOOD SQUARE
GLASGOW NOVEMBER 1910.

□■ c SOUTH ELEVATION
□□ Pencil, ink and watercolour, 60.5 × 86 cm

47
MACKINTOSH ROOM
Once the Board Room, it now contains part
of the School's collection of furniture and
paintings

all, responsive to any opportunity for an enriching or more intense solution towards the realisation of his buildings which defies any rational explanation.

In the very fertility of his imagination lies an important contemporary issue for design, the understanding of the importance of choice, of the need for change, even for whimsy (what might be called the Milan Syndrome[5]). This recognises the importance of fashion for society and for industry, utilising the machine's ability for effortlessly re-shaping as production runs finish; there is the potential for satisfying the need for strengthening personal identity through exercised personal choice of individual artefacts. The scope of Mackintosh's achievement in this respect can be seen in the School of Art, not only in the building form itself, but also in his artistic transformations of chairs, tables, roof trusses, staircases, towel rails, stools, and even the ubiquitous artist's easel. Equally relevant and now being recognised in the ambience of the Post-Modern ethos, was his astonishing architectural ability to create, through detailing, singular building 'events', or to define particular spaces through simple arrangements of building elements, a truss, a doorway or a window embrasure; or to orchestrate unforgettable sequences of low and high, dark and light, closed and open spaces. All this can be seen in the widest possible way in this huge, complex, yet reassuring build-ing which was Mackintosh's biggest executed commission and his greatest achievement.

These are some of the aspects of his work, which, for today's architects and designers, conscious of the sterility of the purely quantitative approach of the last fifty years, offer thought and inspiration for them in their search to rediscover their individual and artistic roles as makers of form, and of place. At this level, Mackintosh's working methods are of par-ticular interest and close study of the School reveals in some measure how he was able to let a building achieve its particu-lar identity, yet be a vehicle for a virtuoso display of his per-sonal talent.

Throughout the building he demonstrates a creative exploitation of each and every specific requirement, seizing

51
Charles R. Mackintosh
THE GLASGOW SCHOOL OF ART/
PROPOSED ALTERATIONS EXTENSIONS,
1907
A selection from a set of eleven drawings
dealing with phase 2, all drawn at 4
Blythswood Square
Glasgow School of Art

a No 1 NEW ENTRESOL FORMED
BETWEEN BASEMENT AND GROUND
FLOORS ▫▪
▫

b PLAN OF SUB-BASEMENT, April
Ink and watercolour, 58 × 80.5 cm

c No 2 PLAN OF BASEMENT FLOOR,
October 1st ▫▫
▪
Ink and watercolour, 58 × 86.3 cm
The extensions are indicated by a wash

the opportunity to create an architectural 'event' through some feat of invention. His design strategy and working method emerge from study of the primary architectural object, the building itself, and comparison with such existing documentation as the drawings and the conditions and brief for the competition from which it emerged.

Clearly after the initial strategic distribution of the accommodation, i.e. the basic plans and sections were completed, each part of the building was then subjected to examination and re-examination as detail design or building work proceeded, a process of tactical confrontation with the potential of each particular situation. This is an adaptive and responsive strategy, which demands a constant holistic awareness of the unique and the possible, a process which, inevitably, has resulted in a built form of such complexity as to make comprehension or description difficult.

Few though the remaining drawings are, comparison with the building as executed not only reveals something of the process but in their explicitness make clear Mackintosh's planning ability and his interest in the use of contemporary technology. Reading the newly rediscovered, rather explicit Competition Conditions and brief confirms this interpretative view of Mackintosh's architectural approach given above, a view which perhaps helps explain why both the High Modern and the Post-Modern Movements continue simultaneously to derive insight, inspiration and confirmation from direct experience or study of the School of Art.

The brilliantly simple organisation of the plan is derived directly from the Conditions of the Competition,[6] then developed in the third dimension. The E-shaped plan has a maximised street frontage on three sides and, concealing some complexity at the rear, a short sensible internal circulation serves a lineal arrangement of subdividable, north-facing studios; the rooms of special use or volume or shape occur at the ends and in the centre; a recognition of the specialness of position; of 'end quality', terminal, lit on two or more sides; and of 'the middle', the optimum position for entry, here a central stair leads up directly to the museum and the Director's Room — providing immediate information

on the nature of the building and in practical terms is convenient for control of access.

The section of the building is equally direct, superimposed studio floors step out and down at the base to recognise and occupy the whole of the steep site, and expand up into the roof in an exploitation of the possibilities of 'the top', in a multiplicity of roof-lit rooms. The section is in effect an exploration of the interaction of structure and the special kinds of light available: 'steady, north light' in the studios for painting, 'warm sunlight' in the circulation spaces, the 'toplit' basement area encouraging the penetration of light deep into the sculpture studios of the basement floor, themselves logically located there for simple reasons of weight.

Essentially simple, this *parti*[7] is transformed in realisation at an architectural level into a wonderful, sophisticated sequence of horizontal and vertical, tactile and spatial experiences which has been described elsewhere in considerable detail.[8] Plans and sections respond to use, materials and construction condition execution, from these basic rules buildings are conceived, but what raises any building to the status of architecture is the level of social expectation involved in its genesis, and the understanding and skill of the designer in its development. In 1896, the Governors of the School demanded a plain and suitable building, but necessarily were involved in the spending of public money on a large and specialised building for public use; expectation of some reasonable architectural quality was implicit. Mackintosh was not found lacking.

The School's importance in his day lay in its manifest rejection of 'stylism', in its demonstration of the possibility of an architecture having its sole genesis in its use and its construction, moderated by the contingencies of its location. It can be seen to have helped direct the Modern Movement towards its later programmatic development. Now it is seen as a prime example of a building conceived at that historic time of transition when the existential nature of architectural form was first recognised, explored and exploited, 'made demonstrative', to use Reyner Banham's phrase in *Theory and Design in the First Machine Age* (1960). A paradox

THE GLASGOW SCHOOL ᵒf ART
PROPOSED ALTERATIONS & EXTENSIONS

Nᵒ 1

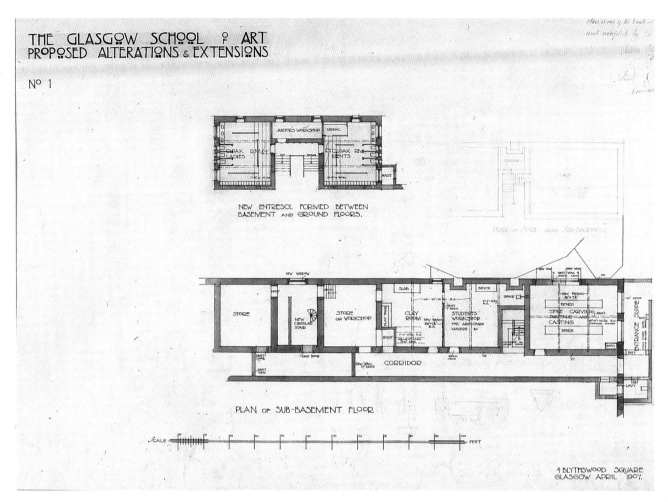

NEW ENTRESOL FORMED BETWEEN
BASEMENT and GROUND FLOORS.

PLAN of S'PIRE over SUB-BASEMENT

PLAN of SUB-BASEMENT FLOOR

SCALE ⊢⊢⊢⊢⊢⊢⊢⊢⊢⊢⊢⊢⊢⊢⊢⊢ FEET

4 BLYTHSWOOD SQUARE
GLASGOW APRIL 1907.

THE GLASGOW SCHOOL ᵒf ART
PROPOSED ALTERATIONS EXTENSIONS

Nᵒ 2

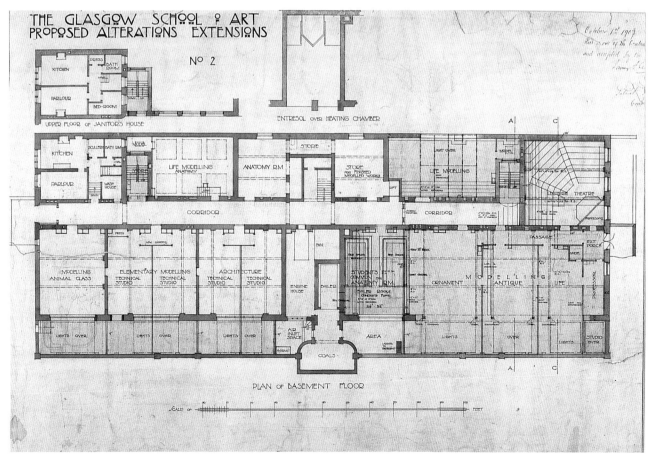

UPPER FLOOR of JANITOR'S HOUSE

ENTRESOL OVER HEATING CHAMBER

PLAN of BASEMENT FLOOR

SCALE of ⊢⊢⊢⊢⊢⊢⊢⊢⊢⊢⊢⊢ FEET

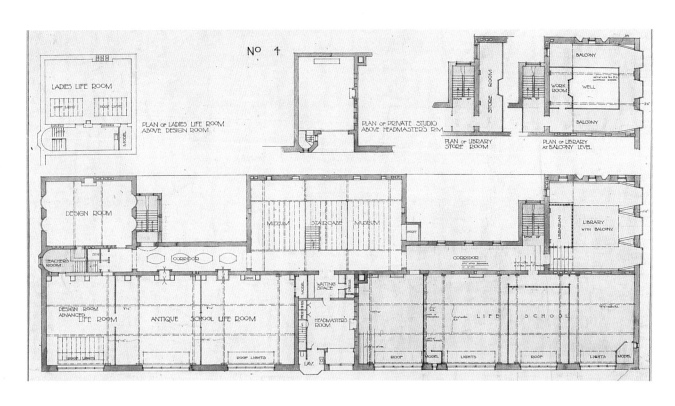

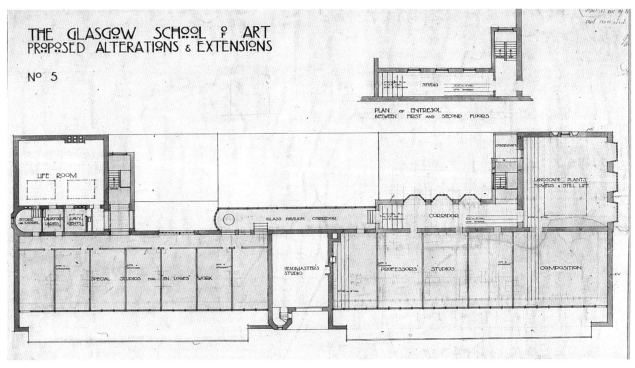

THE GLASGOW SCHOOL ᵒғ ART
PROPOSED ALTERATIONS & EXTENSIONS

Nº 6

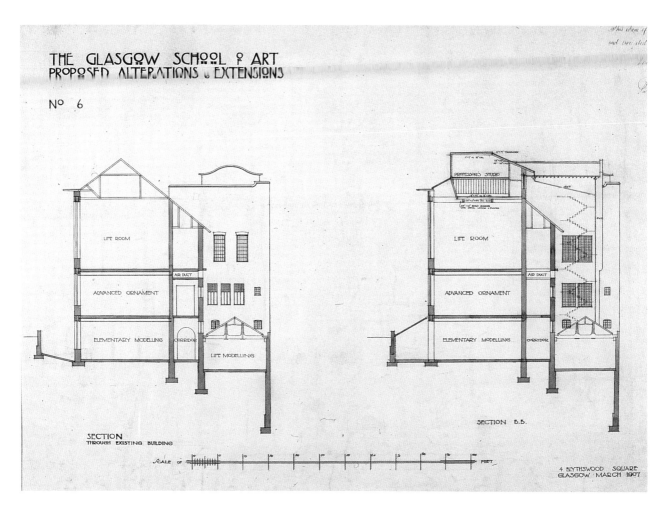

LIFE ROOM

ADVANCED ORNAMENT

AIR DUCT

ELEMENTARY MODELLING CORRIDOR LIFE MODELLING

SECTION
THROUGH EXISTING BUILDING

PROFESSOR'S STUDIO

LIFE ROOM

ADVANCED ORNAMENT

AIR DUCT

ELEMENTARY MODELLING CORRIDOR

SECTION B.B.

SCALE OF ————— FEET

4 BLYTHSWOOD SQUARE
GLASGOW. MARCH. 1907

THE GLASGOW SCHOOL ᵒғ ART
PROPOSED ALTERATIONS & EXTENSIONS

Nº 7

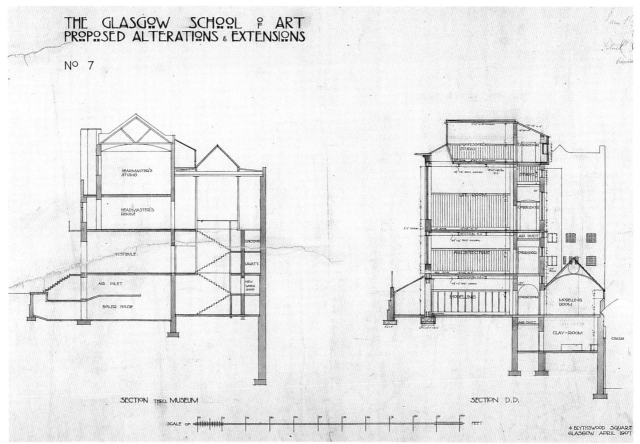

HEADMASTER'S STUDIO

HEADMASTER'S ROOM

VESTIBULE

AIR INLET

BOILER HOUSE

JUNCTION

LAVATY

NEW WORK SHOP

SECTION THRO. MUSEUM

PROFESSOR'S STUDIO CORRIDOR

STUDIO

LIFE ROOM CORRIDOR

AIR DUCT

ARCHITECTURE CORRIDOR

MODELLING CORRIDOR MODELLING ROOM

AIR DUCT

CLAY-ROOM CIRCUS

SECTION D.D.

SCALE OF ————— FEET

4 BLYTHSWOOD SQUARE
GLASGOW. APRIL. 1907

h No 8 SECTION ON LINE CC, SECTION
ON LINE A A , April
Ink and watercolour, 58 × 91 cm
Outline of the Library interior

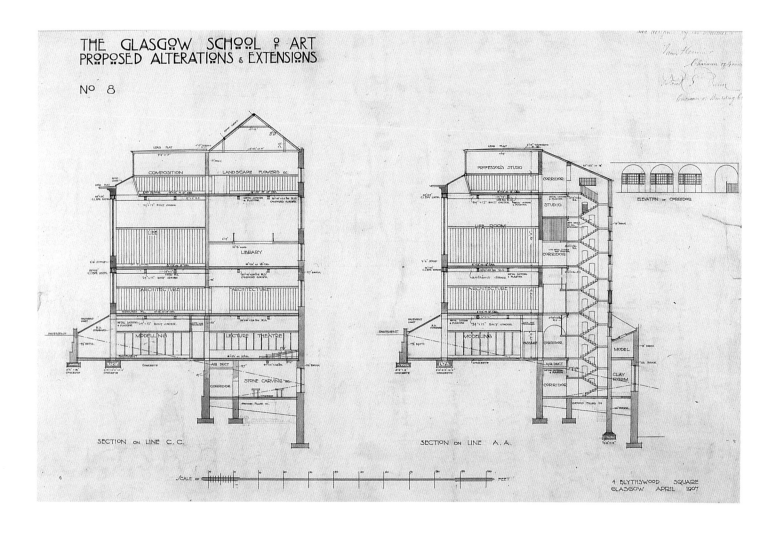

52
Charles R. Mackintosh
TWO DRAWINGS FROM A SET OF TEN
November, 1910
See also nos 46, 82
Glasgow School of Art

a SECTION A A, SECTION D D
Ink and watercolour, 60.5 × 80.5 cm

b SECTION C C, SECTION D D
Ink and watercolour, 68 × 80.5 cm

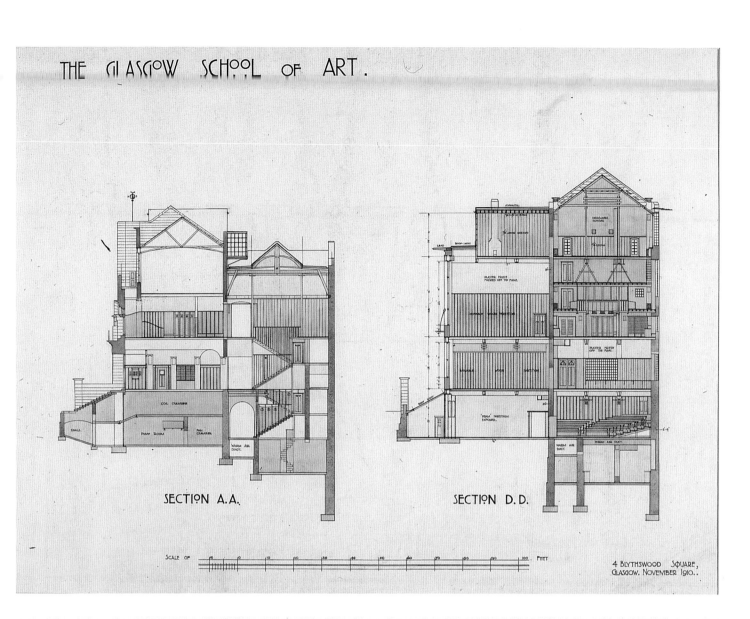

SECTION A.A.

SECTION D.D.

SCALE OF _____ FEET

4 BLYTHSWOOD SQUARE,
GLASGOW. NOVEMBER 1910.

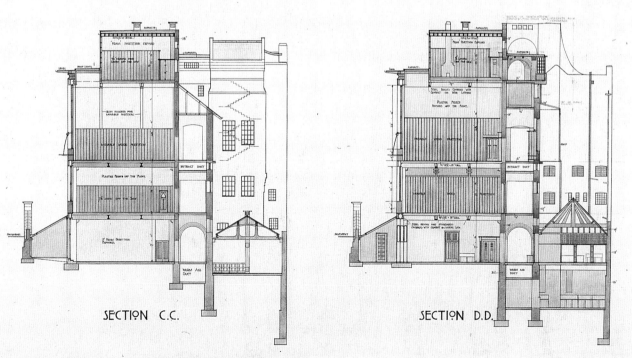

SECTION C.C.

SECTION D.D.

of reduction and enrichment, nowadays it is as exciting to a generation conditioned by Robert Venturi and Charles Moore, engaged in rediscovering the nature of complexity and contradiction as it was in its own time to a generation determined to throw off the millstone of historicism.

For contemporary urbanists too, Rossi, Norberg-Schultz, Lynch *et al*, Mackintosh and his opus have equal relevance. The social need for identity — that sense of who and where one is, has been rediscovered as a potent factor in urbanism — a sense consciously reinforced by the uniqueness and contingent relevance of those special buildings which by their singularity act as referents in the built environment. As already observed, the School gives a Post-Modern encouragement by its very specificity and Mackintosh's enduring relevance as a designer is enhanced by his continuous demonstration of the importance of invention. Today's architects are fascinated by this grasp of context and contingency and above all by his sensitivity to the niceties of use and place, while today's designers recognise and try to understand and to emulate the power of his objects. Of supreme importance is his holistic comprehension, the ability to enhance the basic programmatic approach (so characteristic of the Modern Movement), by sensitive, inventive, or even obsessive attention to detail, creating both a memorable object, a totality, the building, and an orchestrated symphony of iconic effects. It is this, above all, which today confirms Mackintosh as a major architectural figure and the Glasgow School of Art his masterwork.

NOTES

1   The author has dealt with this in some detail in 'Mackintosh in Context', Patrick Nuttgens (ed.), *Mackintosh and his Contemporaries*, Murray, 1988, pp. 25-31.

2   See for example the photographs of the Art School interior in Bruno Taut, *Modern Architecture, The Studio*, 1929, pp. 44, 45.

3   By 'programmatic' is implied the idea that given the 'programme' for the building, i.e. the number and nature of the rooms, and their inter-relationships, a form will ensue; while the term 'tectonic' means that order which derives from the structural system selected. Mackintosh's contemporaries recognised that these were merely the means to an end and recognised his architectural control and sensibility. Later, the ensuing functionalism became itself the end, and, devoid of sensibility, led to the rejection of modern architecture on a wide scale.

4   Anthony Vidler, 'The Third Typology', *Oppositions*, Winter 1976-7, MIT, p. 2.

5   The Milan Syndrome is a phrase coined to encapsulate the idea that machine production creates the possibility of change (in the need for re-tooling) at the same time as the need for market stimulation creates a demand for fashion. This is best seen at work in the Milan Biennale where manufacturers must show, or perish, and designers become performers.

6   See Appendix A.

7   *Parti* is a useful *Ecole des Beaux-Arts* term meaning organisation of parts, scheme of things.

8   Andrew MacMillan, 'Invention and Identity' in Yukio Futagawa (ed.), *Charles Rennie Mackintosh: The Glasgow School of Art*, A.D.A., Edita, Tokyo, 1979.

53
LIBRARY, c. 1980
Photograph
Light and Shade

A TOUR
OF THE SCHOOL

ANDREW
MACMILLAN
JAMES
MACAULAY
WILLIAM
BUCHANAN

EXTERIOR

THE School is 245 ft long by 93 ft deep. From street level it is 86 ft high but the slope of the ground behind at the west end adds another 34 feet. It is a large building occupying the whole length of a block in the grid pattern of the city centre. The north, east and west façades are built of Giffnock and Whitespot sandstone in a mixture of ashlar and squared, snecked rubble. The south façade is of brick treated with roughcast. The plan is E shaped with three wings projecting to the south.

NORTH FAÇADE

At the centre of the façade, as if to mark its exact position, stands a tapering timber post. From the post, surprisingly, hang two doors — the jambs opposite would have been the expected position. These doors, In and Out, therefore swing in opposing directions creating, when it is busy, an intriguing sense of movement like a piece of kinetic sculpture. Each door has a square window with a frame, below which are two small leaves in glass, all joined to a stalk which ends in a seed

54
RELIEF CARVING ABOVE ENTRANCE

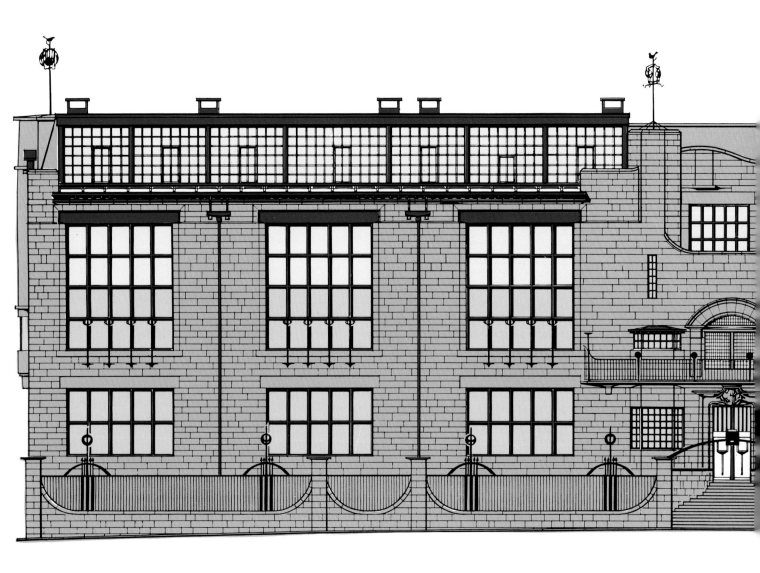

form at the bottom. However, plans and elevations dated November 1910[1] do not show these doors at all, only the present set of inner doors. This makes better sense of the delightful wicket on the left, its window pierced with nine squares, which was slid upwards by the Janitor to deal immediately with inquirers before entering the building itself. At present the wicket is closed for the space between the two sets of doors does not allow this arrangement to function with any comfort.

The façade clearly displays what happens behind: a solid central section houses the entrance and administration; on either side glazed sections hold the studios. The

façade is set out from the central door post in a beautiful scheme of balanced asymmetry. While the entrance is in the centre of the façade it is asymmetrically placed within the central section.[2] Above the entrance a board announces the name of the building and its number, 167, in Renfrew Street. Set above that is the guardian of the entrance, a carved stone relief (with symmetrically arranged figures) so carefully related to the building that it is impossible to say where sculpture stops and architecture begins.

To the left of the entrance is the bay window of the Janitor's original office. Above is another bay. Mackintosh drew such arrangements of windows during his trips to

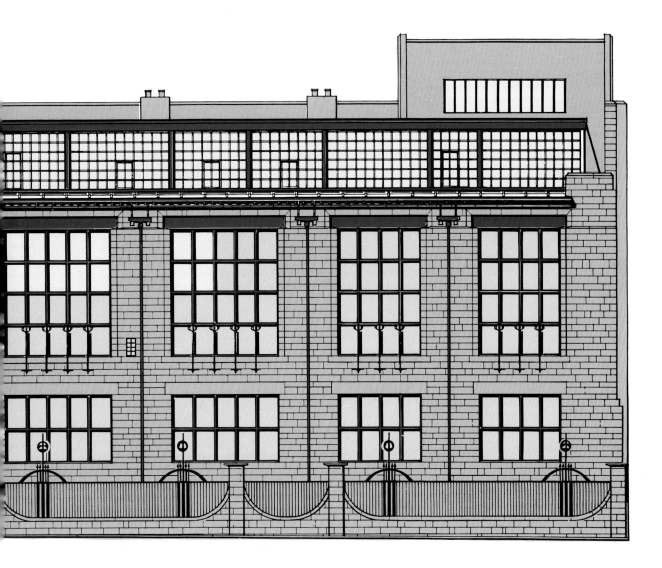

England, e.g. at Chipping Campden in 1894,[3] or in Lyme Regis in 1895.[4] The double bay window, one above the other, was also being used by C. F. A. Voysey. Voysey's treatment of a triple bay, in a house for the Earl of Lovelace, was illustrated in the *British Architect* in July 1895. That issue also contained the Honeyman & Keppie Canal Boatmen's Institute and Mackintosh's design for its clock face.

The first floor of the central section contains the office of the Director whose accommodation also occupies the rest of this section. The importance of this suite and its occupant (felt personally, no doubt, by Mackintosh in relation to Newbery) is prominently marked by the outside balcony running along its length (although there is no record of a Director ever having used the balcony to address the student body crowded in the street beneath). This composition of balcony, bay window and arched window bears a resemblance to J. M. MacLaren's house at 10-12 Palace Court, Bayswater, London, 1889-90.[5] The School's bay window contains not, as might be expected, the Director's desk but, perversely, his lavatory. It is the arched window with the stone transom which lights the Director's office. The slit window above lights the staircase to the studio. This is set back behind a walled balcony which can be entered only from the stair. It is extremely fortress-like. Above the Director's studio window, on a ledge,

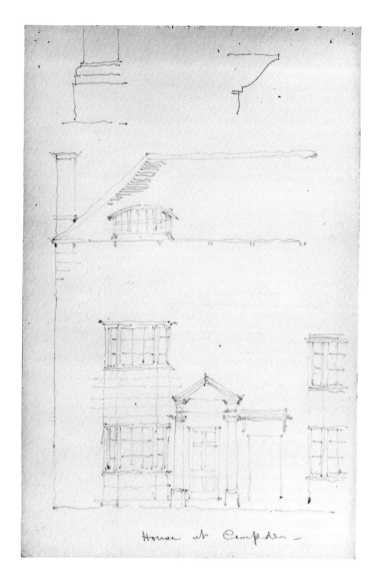

House at Campden

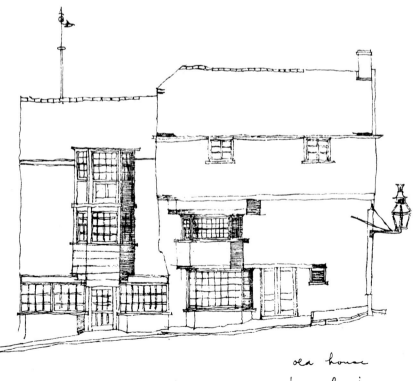

old house
Lyme Regis

56
Charles R. Mackintosh
■□ HOUSE AT CAMPDEN, 1894
Pencil, 17.8 × 11.6 cm
Hunterian Art Gallery, University of Glasgow,
Mackintosh Collection

57
J. M. MacLaren
□■ 10-12 PALACE COURT, BAYSWATER,
LONDON, 1889-90
Detail from an ink-photo by Sprague & Co
From the Architectural Illustration Society,
2nd Series, no 407, in the *Architect*, 22 July
1892
Mitchell Library, Glasgow

58
Charles R. Mackintosh
□□ OLD HOUSE, LYME REGIS, 1895
■
Pencil, 26 × 20.4 cm
Reproduced in 'Sketchbook Jottings' in the
British Architect, 29 November 1895
Mitchell Library, Glasgow

59
MACKINTOSH BUILDING
FROM THE NEWBERY TOWER □■
This shows clearly the central portion which
contains the entrance, the Director's balcony,
and above it the studio with a slated roof

is a plain stone panel which, in a preliminary drawing, is shown carved with the city's coat of arms. However, a three-dimensional wrought-iron tree and bird from the city's arms stands on top of the tower to announce that this is the School of Art in *Glasgow.*

From each side of this section stretch the studios. They are part of the scheme of subtle, carefully balanced asymmetry. Three studios with windows five panes wide lie to the east. Four studios lie to the west, but, within this group, two of the studios have windows five panes wide, and two studios (the westernmost) have windows four panes wide. A tiny window (to light a model's changing-room) adds a sharp change in scale and proclaims the thickness of the wall.

The huge first-floor studio windows are braced firmly by metal brackets on which, until the 1960s, window cleaners laid planks to rest their ladders. The brackets are in the form of plants, their heads drawn back against the glass. The three sets of brackets to the east record the growth of a seed. Starting from the centre, the first set of brackets has stamen-like forms in the centres of their heads. The next set has a small seed in each head. In the final set each head contains a full, round seed. The brackets on the windows to the west have flower-like heads, though they do not seem to express a similar idea of growth. These brackets, clearly examples of 'decorated construction' which would have pleased both Pugin and Ruskin, relieve the otherwise severely plain façade. Sometimes they cast shadows on the façade. Sometimes they are seen mirrored in the studio windows. They can also be enjoyed from inside the studios, silhouetted against the sky.

In contrast to the façade, the wall and railings along the street are symmetrical, though the sequence of the Japanese-like symbols on their stalks above the railings is not. The railings cast interesting shadows on the upward curve of the stone walls at the ends of each section. This arrangement is similar to the railings of Smith & Brewer's Passmore Edwards Settlement (later Mary Ward House), Tavistock Place, London, of 1895, especially the side elevation to Little Coram Street (no longer extant).[6]

Hidden from the street by the flat overhanging roof are the attic studios, added at the second phase of building. The chimneys on the western section mark five staff studios each with a fireplace which gives these spaces a decidedly domestic atmosphere in contrast to the larger, public, areas of the School. The studio and fireplace of the Director are grandest of all. Those of the Head of Painting are grander than the rest.

64
MacGibbon & Ross
CRATHES CASTLE: View from the South-West
Drawing from *Castellated and Domestic Architecture of Scotland,*
vol 2, 1887, p. 111
Glasgow School of Art Library

65
Charles R. Mackintosh
MERRIOTT CHURCH, SOMERSET, 1895
Pencil, 36.2 × 12.7 cm
The drawing extends across two pages of Mackintosh's sketchbook
Hunterian Art Gallery, University of Glasgow, Mackintosh Collection

EAST FAÇADE

The façade shown on a drawing of September 1897 was modified when built. Most noticeably the gable wall to the north was levelled and the dovecot, shown set into this wall, became a small house complete with landing pad perched on the edge of the wall. With false entrances, no nesting boxes, nor easy access for anyone wishing to feed the birds in frosty weather, its function must therefore be symbolical, another reference to nature. Beneath the dovecot the huge expanse of wall was to have been relieved by three trees planted at its foot. They would have acted as a fine foil by casting moving shadows on the large flat surface. However the ground is now so full of gas, electrical and water services that it would be difficult to replace these without major upheaval.

In the southern portion of this façade, again in asymmetrical balance, are disposed a set of windows and a tower embedded in the façade. The tower may owe its origins to a similar arrangement on the south face of Crathes Castle as shown in MacGibbon and Ross.[7] However, Mackintosh's tower is octagonal, more like the one which he drew in 1895 at the church in Merriott in Somerset, though that starts at ground level.

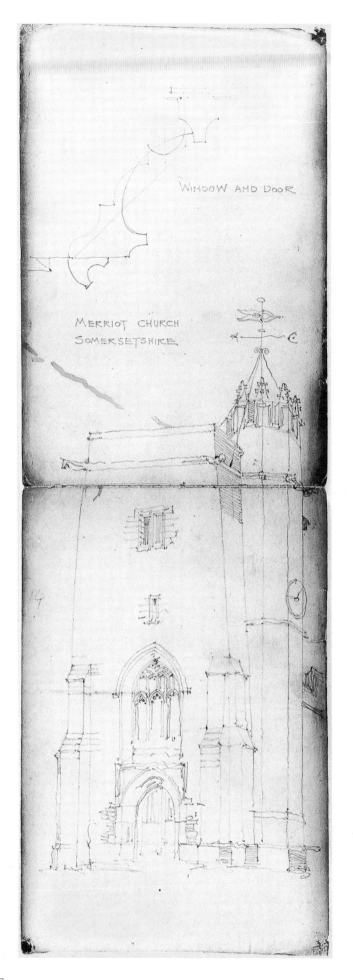

WINDOW AND DOOR

MERRIOT CHURCH
SOMERSETSHIRE

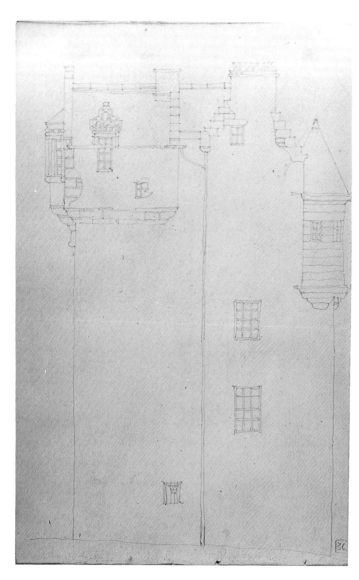

66
Charles R. Mackintosh
MAYBOLE CASTLE, AYRSHIRE, 1895
Pencil, 17.6 × 11.5 cm
Hunterian Art Gallery, University of Glasgow, Mackintosh Collection

67
MacGibbon & Ross
MAYBOLE CASTLE, from South-West
From *Castellated and Domestic Architecture of Scotland,* vol 3, 1889, p. 500
Glasgow School of Art Library

The lowest window in the School tower may have been inspired by the oriel window at Maybole Castle which Mackintosh also drew in 1895, showing it in elevation. It also appears in MacGibbon and Ross.[8] The Maybole Castle oriel rests on corbelling but Mackintosh's window, shaded by a projecting cornice, and the tower above it, are supported by one huge corbel stone. The oriel is an unusual feature in Scottish vernacular architecture, though not in tenements in Glasgow. Above, the narrow window lights the School wardrobe which once held the objects and garments used for painting. The small window above that lights the ladder to the top of the tower. The tower is a splendid vantage point for viewing the city set in its basin, and, 30 miles to the south-west, the Tinto Hills, or, north 25 miles where the Highlands begin. Planted on the tower is another version of the city's

coat of arms, its tree much fuller than the one on the Director's tower and with a round seed inside it. Again the idea of growth and the fullness of nature is expressed.

The area to the south of the tower is composed of a pattern of windows. The two bottom rows of rectangular, Voysey-like windows light what was once the Janitor's accommodation. Above these the arched window from the Director's office on the north façade reappears. Next to it is the tiny window of a W.C. Above are two tall curved windows sharing a common lintel — relating, perhaps, to the two curved windows on Voysey's house at 12-14 Hans Road, London, 1892. With a similar pair on the other side, these windows flood the original Board Room. At the summit the ends of this wall are swept up in a treatment which can be seen in an illustration of Voysey's Hans Road houses in the *Builder* of September

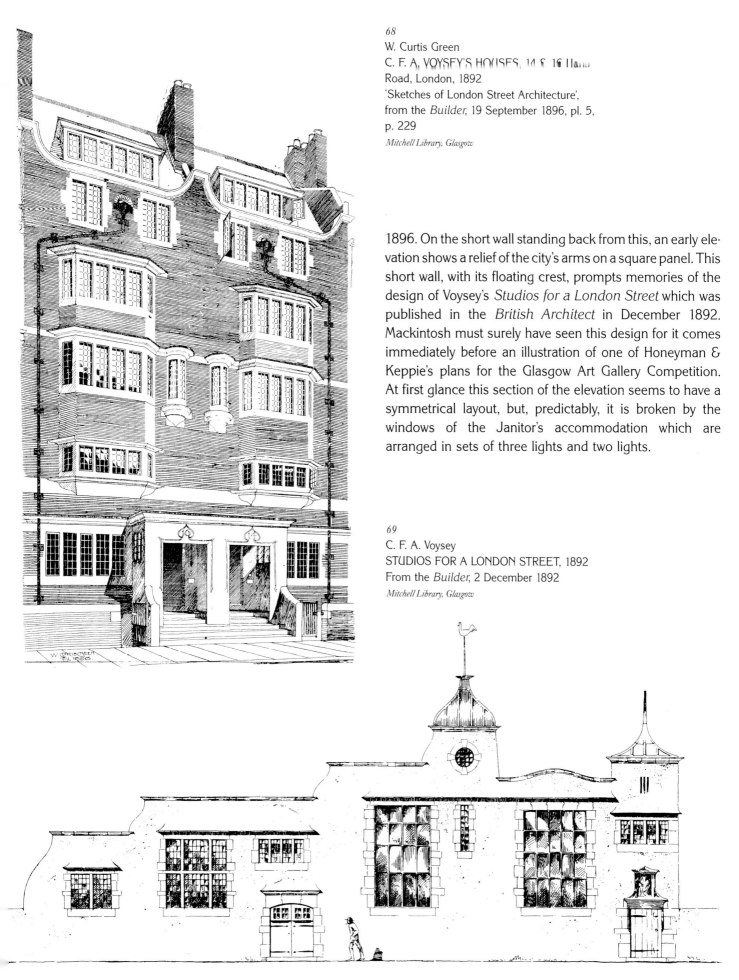

68
W. Curtis Green
C. F. A. VOYSEY'S HOUSES, 14 & 16 Hans
Road, London, 1892
'Sketches of London Street Architecture',
from the *Builder*, 19 September 1896, pl. 5,
p. 229
Mitchell Library, Glasgow

1896. On the short wall standing back from this, an early elevation shows a relief of the city's arms on a square panel. This short wall, with its floating crest, prompts memories of the design of Voysey's *Studios for a London Street* which was published in the *British Architect* in December 1892. Mackintosh must surely have seen this design for it comes immediately before an illustration of one of Honeyman & Keppie's plans for the Glasgow Art Gallery Competition. At first glance this section of the elevation seems to have a symmetrical layout, but, predictably, it is broken by the windows of the Janitor's accommodation which are arranged in sets of three lights and two lights.

69
C. F. A. Voysey
STUDIOS FOR A LONDON STREET, 1892
From the *Builder*, 2 December 1892
Mitchell Library, Glasgow

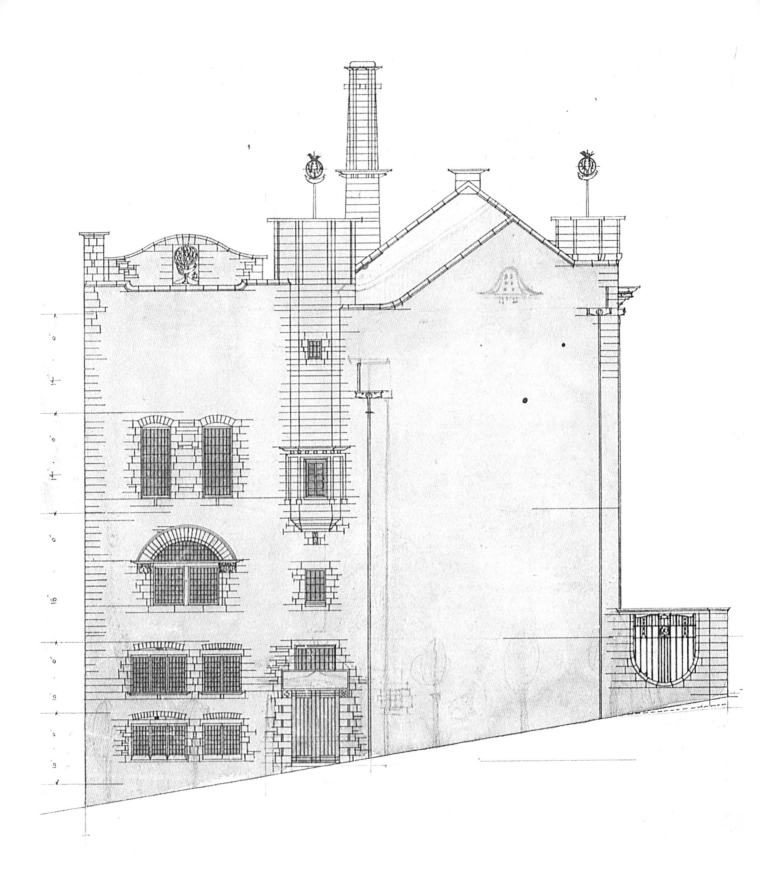

70
Charles R. Mackintosh
EAST ELEVATION, 1897
Detail from drawing no 6 of the east and west elevations
Pencil, ink and watercolour, 55.5 × 91 cm
Drawn at 140 Bath Street in March   *Glasgow School of Art*

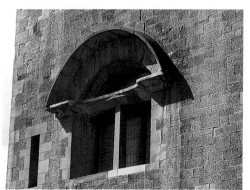

73
FINIAL ON TOP OF EAST TOWER □ ■
Wrought iron, 224 × 76 cm

SOUTH FAÇADE

This is treated unashamedly as the back of the building. The façade may have a cheaper, roughcast finish, but it is none-theless carefully designed. Extending from the length of the building are three wings. That to the east contains the orig-inal Board Room. To this wing was added a staircase at the time of the second phase of building thus allowing the east-ern internal stair to be removed. In the inset between this wing and the next is the top-lit Anatomy studio. Above is a group of three windows to light the ground-floor corridor, then there are three inlets for the heating system, and, in the sloping roof, the three skylights which light the first-floor cor-ridor and its collection of casts. Higher still are the windows of the upper corridor, and over them the tiny windows which are set high in the wall of the attic studios.

The centre wing has a pattern of windows of class rooms and offices. It houses the main staircase and the top-lit Museum. Over the Museum roof a glass-enclosed passageway was built out on brackets to connect the first phase of the building with the second, since the height of the Director's Studio cut off access, at this level, between the old and new parts of the building. In the next inset is a top-lit Modelling studio. The wall above it contains the three ground-floor corridor windows, three inlets, and then three tall windows to light the corridor to the Library. Next to them are the three windows of a long and narrow mezzanine room. Over these are three oriel windows marking the top of the wall. These may well have been based on three similar windows on the south front of Huntly Castle illustrated in MacGibbon and Ross.[10]

The western wing contains in the sub-basement the original stone-carving studio with access from the side street; in the basement the Lecture Theatre; on the ground floor, the old Architecture School; above it, the two floors of the Library; then the Library store; and finally a large top-lit studio. A greenhouse, important at that time for providing flowers for drawing, is cantilevered on a steel beam over a dizzy space. The treatment of the windows is especially inter-

74
MacGibbon & Ross
HUNTLY CASTLE, from the South
From *Castellated and Domestic Architecture
of Scotland*, vol 2, 1887, p. 280
Glasgow School of Art Library

esting in their relation to the interiors for the window below the top window serves two separate spaces, the Library balcony and the store above it. All windows lie within the thickness of the wall, in contrast to the projecting windows of the neighbouring west façade.

In sharp contrast to the asymmetry of the northern façade, all the features in each of the sections at the rear of this building are arranged in symmetrical groups.

WEST FAÇADE

When the money was raised for the second phase of the building the whole west wing was re-designed. The first undistinguished elevation, not unlike the east façade, was transformed. It became a bold, exciting and inspiring statement speaking confidently of the future. It is the work of a mature architect beginning the process of abstraction which was to be continued in the Modern Movement.

The front doorway to the School had received very special treatment, and so did the western doorway. It is an exercise in recession and projection with the door surround being pulled forward while the wall behind is hollowed out. The top portion of the keystone is, like a Mannerist conceit, removed and round the doorway is a stepped hood anticipating the lines of art deco. The door leads to the basement and, immediately on the right, to the Lecture Theatre so that there is no need to use the longer route via the front door.

The west façade is superbly composed, playing off the dressed stone of the window area against the rough stone of the studio wall. The line of demarcation between these areas is expressed above the row of ground floor windows by the tiniest setback of the entire façade, most clearly observed at the north-west corner of the building.

Dominating this façade are the three bays of the Library. These extend upwards to the top of the wall where they hold three horizontal windows. They extend downwards to hold the three windows of the former Architecture studios. The long Library windows, 25 ft high, standing above voids, niches in the centre of the bay, are richly treated. They are outlined by stone mouldings (a device prominent at Crathes Castle, see fig. 64) which move only by turning at right angles or by being stepped. These mouldings also enclose the roughly dressed stone drums, one at either side of each window, which were to be carved. The Library windows and the ground-floor windows project from the façade thus extending their spaces. Once again a tiny window is cut into the wall, this time as if to emphasise the height of the Library windows.[11]

76
WEST DOORWAY

The windows once had iron frames to hold the 9-in. squares of glass, but these were replaced in 1947 by thicker bronze frames. There are visual delights in using small panes of glass, for, depending on the light, in some places they are transparent, in other places they appear solid, they reflect the light, they catch other reflections, they sparkle in the sun. How different from the large, placid, mirror-like studio panes of the north façade.

Set back from the top of this façade is a triangular gable in which is cut a channel as if to mark the apex of the School.

77
T & R Annan
WEST DOORWAY n d ◻∎
Photograph
T & R Annan and Sons Ltd, Glasgow

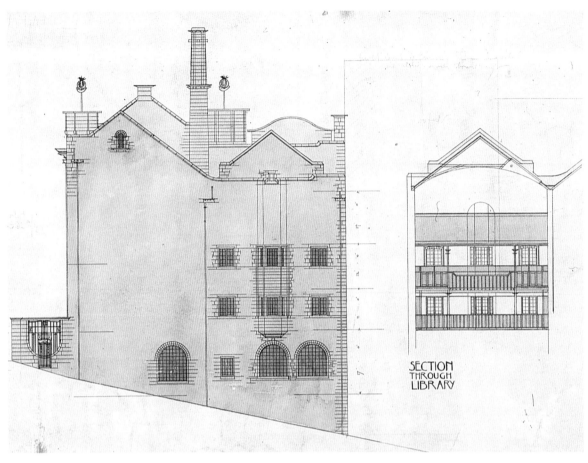

SECTION
THROUGH
LIBRARY

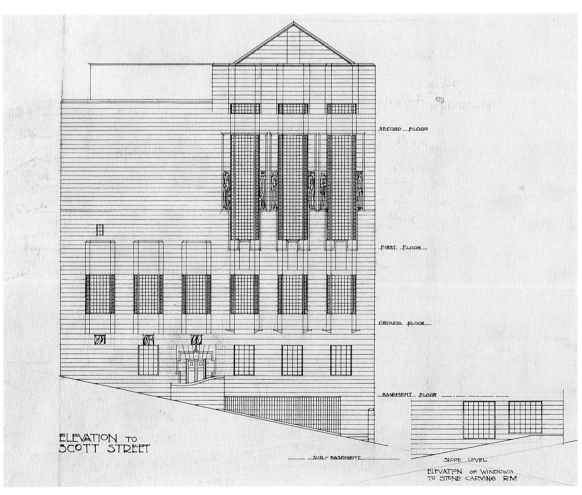

SECOND FLOOR

FIRST FLOOR

GROUND FLOOR

BASEMENT FLOOR

ELEVATION TO
SCOTT STREET

SUB-BASEMENT

SLOPE LEVEL

ELEVATION OF WINDOWS
TO STONE CARVING RM

82
Charles R. Mackintosh
FIVE DRAWINGS FROM A SET OF TEN,
November, 1910
See also nos 46, 52
Glasgow School of Art

a PLAN OF SECOND FLOOR
Ink and watercolour, 68 × 80 cm

b PLAN OF FIRST FLOOR
Ink and watercolour, 60.8 × 110 cm

c PLAN OF GROUND FLOOR
Pencil, ink and watercolour, 60.5 × 89 cm

d PLAN OF BASEMENT FLOOR
Ink and water-colour, 59.5 × 90.5 cm

e PLAN OF SUB-BASEMENT FLOOR
Ink and water-colour, 58 × 85.5 cm

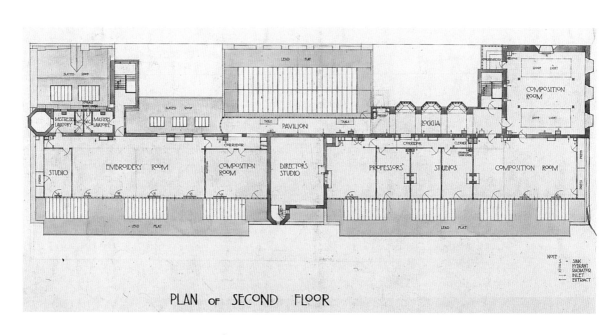

PLAN of SECOND FLOOR

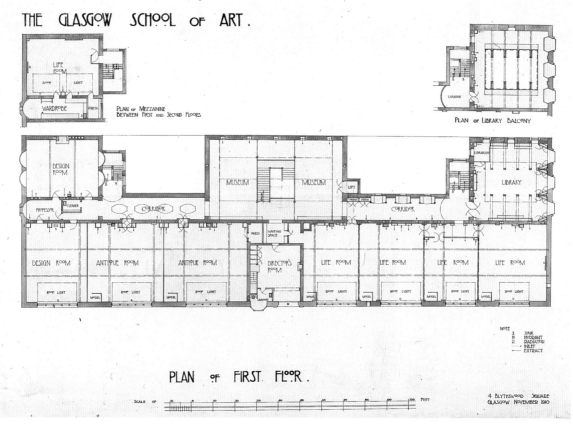

THE GLASGOW SCHOOL of ART.

PLAN of FIRST FLOOR.

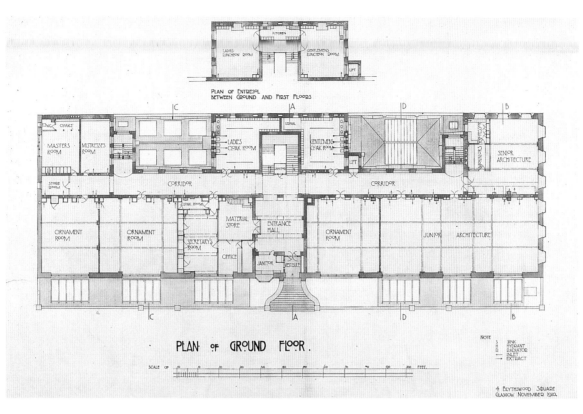

PLAN OF ENTRESOL
BETWEEN GROUND AND FIRST FLOORS

PLAN OF GROUND FLOOR.

SCALE OF FEET.

NOTE
S SINK
H HYDRANT
R RADIATOR
→ INLET
→ EXTRACT

4 BLYTHSWOOD SQUARE
GLASGOW NOVEMBER 1910.

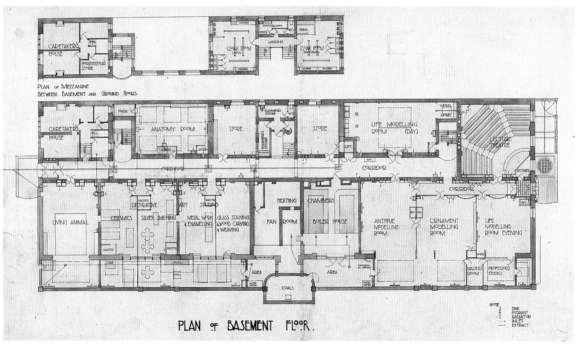

PLAN OF MEZZANINE
BETWEEN BASEMENT AND GROUND FLOORS

PLAN OF BASEMENT FLOOR.

NOTE
S SINK
H HYDRANT
R RADIATOR
→ INLET
→ EXTRACT

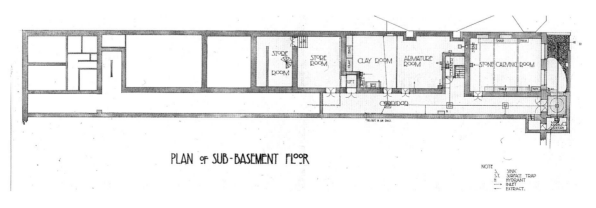

PLAN OF SUB-BASEMENT FLOOR

NOTE
S SINK
S.T. SURFACE TRAP
H HYDRANT
→ INLET
→ EXTRACT.

INTERIOR

Though the interior of the School has 'a kind of space that is undeniably modern',[12] later fire regulations have necessitated the insertion of doors at the beginning and end of corridors, and other additions. Once these spaces would have flowed uninterruptedly into each other. Balconies have also been added to some of the Painting studios.

ENTRANCE HALL

From the street, the wide staircase funnels through the narrow entrance with its two sets of doors into a vaulted Hall. People are drawn onwards, attracted to the light ahead flooding down the central stairwell. The Hall is dark, though it would have been much lighter had the Janitor's bay window not been hidden behind a wall. In the Hall the vaults, almost Piranesian in their weightiness, bear down on solid square piers which mark out a series of interconnected cells. As the Hall is both passageway and meeting place, three benches were designed for people waiting there.

84
T & R Annan
GROUND FLOOR EAST CORRIDOR
Photograph, negative no 14847
To the right is the Inquiry Box. A Janitor in
skipped cap stands to attention. At the end of
the vista is a triangular glass inset in a door
Glasgow School of Art Library

86
COAT-OF-ARMS OF GLASGOW ▫■▫
Wrought iron, length 127 cm
The fish and the bird are later replacements

87
MUSEUM ▫▫■
On the walls is an exhibition of work by staff
in the School of Fine Art

85
BUTTERFLY
Stained-glass, height 45 cm
This is in the door which stops the vista in
the photograph on the left

GROUND-FLOOR CORRIDOR

The corridor runs the length of the floor. The vista to the east
is terminated by a door in which is set a glass panel of a
moth or butterfly.[13] The vista to the west is of two very large
doors, again with glass insets, the entrance to what was the
Architecture School. Other doors in this corridor have
wooden cornices shaped like the external stone transom of
the Director's window. The ceiling joists are left exposed
in the economical manner of Scottish vernacular building.

MAIN STAIRCASE ·

At the foot of the staircase, the Janitor's box, propped out into the central void, is strategically placed to deal with inquiries, and to oversee comings and goings.

The stairwell is defined by three pairs of tall and tapering vertical posts similar to those on the Century Guild's Stand by Arthur Mackmurdo in 1886. The first pair, to the south, starts at basement level and runs up to the level of the Museum balcony. Each post is gripped by double brackets at the floor level of the Museum. The second pair, to the north, starts at ground-floor level and runs up to the roof. The third pair, to the south, starts from the half-landing and also runs to the roof. The treatment of the newel changes as it ascends. In the basement the newel's wooden panelling is pierced with leaf shapes. From the ground floor the newel is formed by wooden balusters, though one broad baluster in the first section of staircase has a pierced decoration. The balusters on the first section rise to the same level as the handrail on the half-landing. The remaining balusters rise to the level of the handrail of the Museum. Thus, the volume of the central well and how it fits into the volume of the Museum is clearly defined.

HALF-LANDING ·

Off the half-landing were, to the west, the Gentlemen's Luncheon Room, and, to the east, the Ladies'. The Kitchen occupied the narrow space between. Over the stairwell projects a third interpretation in wrought iron of the arms of the city. It is complete with all items associated with the miracles of the city's patron saint, Mungo: a tree, a bird, a fish with a ring in its mouth, and one of his possessions, a bell. This was once badly damaged so the fish and the bird are replacements. It is in the treatment of the tree that there are to be found some of the few whiplash lines characteristic of art nouveau in the School. The coat of arms is on the axis of the centre line of the staircase, on which also lies the opening of the Director's room. On the half-landing, on the same axis, is the carved tablet (a tribute, not a memorial)[14] to James Fleming, Chairman of the Governors, and the man chiefly responsible for raising the money to build the School. The tablet, unveiled on 17 January 1903, was designed by the English sculptor George Frampton, though Mackintosh did design its setting, using burnished steel, a familiar metal used for the ubiquitous fire grate. Frampton's tablet shows, behind Fleming, another version of Glasgow's arms, although the oak trees and the acorns are used here for their more usual symbolism.

MUSEUM

Mackintosh accepted the Competition brief which suggested that the Museum might be 'a feature in connection with the staircase'. An early drawing shows steel trusses in the Museum roof, but it was built with specially designed timber trusses with king posts which have cut into them hearts, a motif from Voysey, and, below them, leaf shapes typical of Mackintosh himself. In fact, each set of trusses in the School has a different treatment. Mackintosh had a specific solution for each place: he deliberately turned his back on standard engineering iron components.

Each of the four posts at the corners of the stairwell is fitted with a flat wooden cap to meet the roof beams. Two pairs of wooden caps, devoid of supporting posts, hang from the beams at the far sides of the well. Mackmurdo's exhibition stand for the Century Guild may have been a source for what Pevsner called 'mortarboard' cappings on these posts. As the roof springs from the north and south walls the primary purpose of the posts is to brace the staircase.

89

89
T. Raffles Davidson
CENTURY GUILD FURNITURE STAND
Arthur Mackmurdo, 1886
Sketch from the *British Architect*, vol 26,
5 Nov. 1886. This stand, at the Liverpool
International Exhibition, was painted a bright
yellow. The connected pair of uprights at the
top of the stand may be the source for the
door architraves in several parts of the
School

Mitchell Library, Glasgow

90
Bedford Lemere
DIRECTOR'S OFFICE, 1910 □■
Photograph, negative no 20762/22
Newbery uses one of the tall-backed
armchairs designed for this room. On the
table, to the right of the life drawing, is the
bell which now hangs from the coat-of-arms
at the top of the central staircase. Lemere's
photograph of the new Board Room shows
the Director's circular table and its matching
set of chairs in use there

Glasgow School of Art Library

88
Bedford Lemere
MUSEUM, 1910
Photograph, negative no 20762/3
The Lift opens into the Museum on the west
wall

Glasgow School of Art Library

DIRECTOR'S ROOMS

Outside the Director's rooms, Mackintosh designed what he labelled on his plan a 'waiting space', and thoughtfully provided it with seats. Any student, or member of staff, waiting in the half dark of this tall space, would certainly be suitably impressed when finally admitted.

After the gloom of the entrance, comes one of Mackintosh's first white interiors, heralding the sparse, considered, interiors of the twentieth century. Yet its roots in Scottish vernacular architecture lie very close to the surface. Here are echoes of the rooms built within the stone walls of Scottish castles. The echo is perhaps clearest in the arched area by the window which corresponds to a castle's deep window embrasures. A fine set of such embrasures reaching to the light through walls 7 ft thick is to be found at Castle Campbell, near Dollar.[15]

The window area and the space behind it locate, precisely, the two main activities carried on within the room. The larger, square area, with its higher ceiling, is for discussion and for this a round table with a set of matching chairs were designed. This space is lit by fittings only recently installed but carefully made from the drawings, dated February 1904, in the Hunterian Art Gallery. The square shades are pierced by four sets of nine squares with the central, vertical row of each set situated on the corner of the light fitting. The cornice of the room sweeps down to the height of the window transom. The arched window, at which Newbery worked, is placed asymmetrically in the vaulted space. In the offset area is the hoist which brought up letters from the Janitor's room beneath to arrive just where the desk, only recently constructed (see p. 105), was to stand.

Newbery, in addition to his teaching, his other duties, and his work with the new building, somehow found time to continue to paint, to photograph and to exhibit. The tight, turning, staircase from office to studio does not, however, allow the passage of large paintings. This problem was solved by cutting a slit in the studio floor so that paintings could be lowered into the waiting space next to the top of the staircase. There would be grave problems if ever a sculptor becomes Director!

22

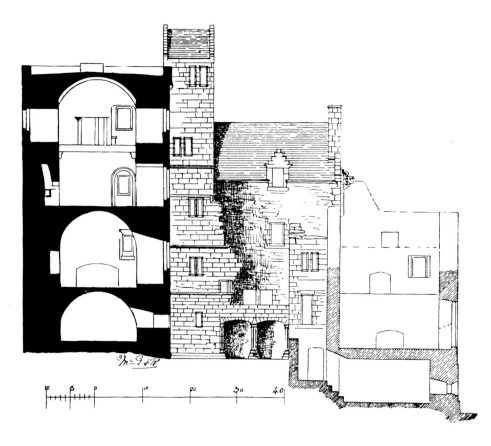

91
MacGibbon & Ross
CASTLE CAMPBELL: Section looking East
From *Castellated and Domestic Architecture
of Scotland*, vol 1, 1887, p. 206
The window embrasures in the castle wall are
like the space in the Director's window
Glasgow School of Art Library

92
DIRECTOR'S OFFICE
With the recent installation of the light-fittings
and the creation of the desk positioned at the
window, the room is only now complete

93
T & R Annan
FIRST FLOOR, East Corridor, looking east
Photograph, negative no 14851
In the first phase of the building the wide
corridors were used for work in the crowded
School
Glasgow School of Art Library

FIRST-FLOOR, EAST CORRIDOR ·

This beautifully top-lit space suggests the vestiges of the
Antique Gallery, a feature of early art schools. On the walls,
and on plinths (and in other corridors), remain some of the
School's huge collection of casts. They are lit from curiously
shaped ogival roof lights which makes this a specific place;
there is no mistaking it for any other corridor in the School.
The plaster ceiling has dark stained timber joists. From each
of these joists, in the second phase of building, a runner was
dropped down the wall to provide a place where casts could
be hung easily.

94
Beford Lemere □■
FIRST FLOOR, East Corridor, looking west,
1910
Photograph, negative no 20762/10
In the second phase of the building the
corridor is used to display casts. With no fire
doors then the length of the corridor could
be enjoyed
Glasgow School of Art Library

17

FIRST-FLOOR, EAST CORRIDOR, STAIRCASE

To reach the added staircase an opening was slapped at floor level through the exterior wall. To create a threshold a steel beam appears to be supported by two wooden posts. Mackintosh's ability to exploit necessity, and by invention subsume it, is clearly demonstrated by the corbelled brick newel which reconciles the different dimensions at the top and bottom of the newel. This treatment also allows a quicker turning. The surface of the staircase is of hard cement, finished with a steel trowel to give a relatively polished surface.

The balcony rail on the half landing above is braced by a metal strap pierced in the Japanese style *Sukashi*. The strap is broad at its bottom but tapering to the point of its contact with the handrail. These parts would have been made off site and assembled *in situ*, an early example of industrial design.

FIRST-FLOOR, WEST CORRIDOR

In contrast to the east corridor, this is lit by three tall windows piercing the south wall. Each window has an accompanying set of built-in seats, sometimes sunny, often used by staff for teaching away from the studios, and occasionally used by students for courting.

95
Bedford Lemere
FIRST FLOOR, East Corridor, Staircase, 1910
Photograph, negative no 20762/17
The corbelling on the newel wall is clearly seen, as is the Board Room windows, once on the outside wall
Glasgow School of Art Library

MACKINTOSH ROOM

This was the Board Room, in which, story has it, the members felt most uncomfortable. This should not have been unexpected if they lived in the tightly cluttered and highly patterned Victorian interiors of the city. Once light poured through pairs of tall windows on both sides into this calm and spacious, white room. Outside, each pair of windows is linked by a common lintel. Inside, they form what has the beginnings of an undulating wall, the outer curves in glass, the inner curve in timber. The distances between the uprights of the wooden panelling and the window uprights are roughly the same bringing a sense of order to the design. On the ceiling of this wonderfully simple space are two steel beams, frankly exposed. Because of the pressure on space in the half-built School, this room soon became a studio. When the second phase of the School was being built a staircase was added to the outside of the west wall across the windows. While the staircase does cut down the light, there is the compensation that the shadows of the steps, and the moving shadows of people as they pass up and down the stairs, can be enjoyed against the opaque glass now in the windows. Here is a creative solution to a difficult problem.

Both doorways in the room have a detached entablature. Both doors contain a glass inset of a seed with roots. Even the heating grilles are treated in a decorative manner. The metal extracts, set in the plaster wall, are quite different from the wooden, slatted, Japanese-like, inputs set low in the panelling of the wall.

Although this room contains a fine collection of furniture, it is also part of a hard-working Art School. Here the Academic Council and its committees use chairs and tables which now may be among the most valuable used by any academic body. It is true that Mackintosh chairs are given a wide berth by those who know that deliberations are to be lengthy, but Mackintosh, who certainly designed furniture for its visual effect, also designed it for a generation who were tailored, corsetted, and taught to sit upright.

96
Bedford Lemere
BOARD ROOM, 1910
Photograph, negative no 20762/9
The room is set up for flower drawing. Some
of this furniture is still in use
Glasgow School of Art Library

97
DOOR IN THE ORIGINAL BOARD ROOM

PAINTING STUDIOS

Along the first floor to the north lie the magnificent Painting studios. To the east two studios, entered by double doors with glass insets of roses, are shown, in a set of plans of October 1910, as Antique Rooms. A set of electric lights on pulleys was provided in these studios so that students could bring a bulb over their working spaces.

The four studios to the west are all marked in 1910 as Life Rooms, though now only the smallest of these is used solely for this purpose. In the old School there had been complaints (common in art schools of that day) about the stuffiness of the gas-lit rooms. Newbery himself mentions this problem, in a letter of 10 February 1922, to John Quinton Pringle, the painter (and optician) and a student at the same time as Mackintosh. Newbery recalled 'the gas-smelling, carbon-laid atmosphere (I can't think of it as "air") of the old Antique Room in Rose Street'. In contrast, Mackintosh created in the new School, airy studios, 30 ft tall, warmed by hot air issuing from grilles in the walls, vented by shafts to the roof, and lit in the evening by electricity which also still drives the studio clocks.

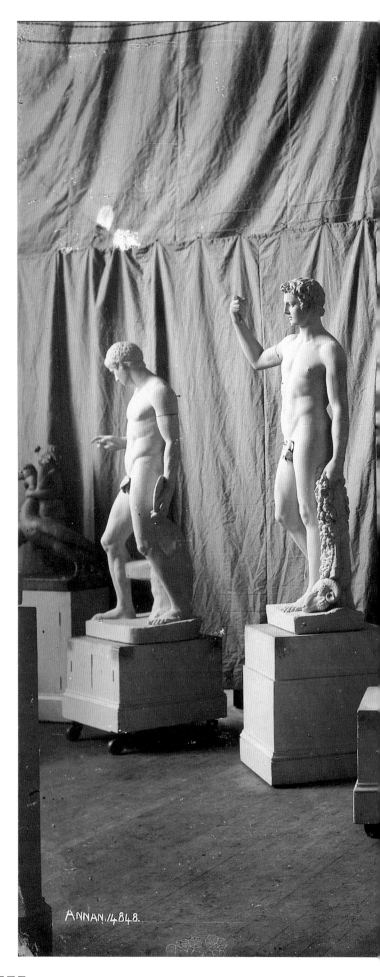

98
T & R Annan
ANTIQUE STUDIO, n d
Photograph, negative no 14848
Mackintosh arranged for the subdivision of this Studio (no 38) by curtains and provided a system for lighting individual work spaces
Glasgow School of Art Library

LIBRARY

Here is the masterpiece within the masterwork, intense, subtle, surprising, and complex. It is a realm of architecture unparallelled then and seldom since. Perhaps the only other comparable space of such intensity is Sir John Soane's house and museum which he built for himself in Lincoln's Inn Fields, London, in 1812.

The Library proper consists of three connected spaces, although only two are, at first, revealed: the Library, its balcony, the store above. It is the ceiling of the store which is the top of the Library space. The store (now the Furniture Gallery) has interior windows which are inverted versions of the external bay windows, forming between them a column of air. Iron brackets from the store's ceiling support its floor and then connect with the posts beneath in the Library itself. The basic layout of the Library depends on the positioning of these posts which rest on steel beams in the floor.

The construction of the posts uses a stick technique, an anticipation of Constructivism, with each post stiffened on both sides with a wooden facing to the point where they meet the double beams which support the balcony. The double beams are pegged on either side of the post.

Had the balcony protruded as far as the posts the area beneath would have been extremely dark, so the line of the balcony was brought back. This gave the opportunity for the decoration of the space between post and balcony with three uprights, chamfered at the angles and painted. Chamfering, a particularly rustic technique, was used by that 'essential Arts and Crafts intellectual' Ernest Gimson.[16] Mackintosh's chamfers are coloured, not with his usual tender violet, pink and purple, but in strong blue, green, red, and white, and in a strict sequence. The symbolic meaning of these colours is a matter for conjecture. Perhaps they stand for the four elements — water, earth, fire and air.

The Library balcony was entered originally from the half-landing on the staircase. Around the top of the balcony runs a narrow undulating strap of steamed timber. On two sides are low cupboards with sloping tops on which books, especially large ones, can be laid for inspection. The balcony afforded an opportunity for inventive decoration. Alternate frontal panels, lightly curved to catch the light, extend below the balcony where each is decorated with a different set of multitudes of tiny oval shapes arranged in columns.

Since the western windows run the entire height of the three-storey Library space, the tops of the windows are much higher than the Library ceiling. One of the most surprising experiences is to look up into these bays, past the balcony, to see revealed the inner windows of the 'secret' store room above. A window in the south wall acts as another link, serving the balcony and the store above where it gives an exciting and steep view to Sauchiehall Street below, and to the city beyond.

Throughout the School Mackintosh took great care with artificial lighting using the comparatively new medium of electricity. His splendid fittings for the thirteen lamps in the centre of the Library suggest a group of suspended miniature skyscrapers.

This powerful room most certainly depends on the construction of its parts and the minimal decoration of these parts for its visual qualities. It also exerts a strong mood, a 'brown study' — almost literally. It is a quiet, sombre, space conducive to study. The Library also derives part of its power from what Lethaby defined as 'cosmical symbolism'. From the high tops of the windows light falls through the Library's many posts in a way that is reminiscent of light filtering down through tall trees. The Library then becomes a small clearing in some quiet northern forest. In the centre of this clearing a great sunburst blazes from the lights suspended from the ceiling. A pale moon-like light comes from the lights placed on the ceiling. Star points shine through the pierced metal fittings under the balcony.

100
■□ CHAMFERS IN THE BALCONY OF THE
LIBRARY

101
□■ CENTRAL LAMPS IN THE LIBRARY, c. 1980

WEST STAIRCASE .

To signal that it is the west staircase, a decoration of rectangular tiles is placed in the walls at its top and in the basement, in addition to the square tile motifs found on both staircases. At the top a particular visual delight awaits. Marking the end of the staircase is a wrought-iron grille, which, though flimsy in comparison, is reminiscent of the yetts (i.e. gates) made of immensely strong interlacing iron which barred the entrance of Scottish tower houses. The top four horizontals of the way through the grille are lengthened so that their ends can be marked with a graphic curve. As the grille has a double roof the inter-action of these two layers of squares can be enjoyed as the spectator moves upwards.

EAST STAIRCASE .

The top of this staircase also has a grille but it is a circular motif which is used in the roof as an aid to location.

STUDIO 58 ·

This beautiful studio sits at the top of the Library tower. Its three western windows, set in embrasures, form the 'eyebrows' of the three tall Library windows. The studio is lit by a south window for it was not designed as a painting studio which demanded constant, even light. It also has two large windows in the roof. No roof trusses are used but a Japanese-like beam construction. The interior of this studio is satisfyingly simple in stone, brick, and timber panels. From the south-east corner the conservatory is entered — by those who have a good head for heights.

103
NUMBER ON DOOR

104
Bedford Lemere
COMPOSITION ROOM, 1910
Photograph, negative no 20762/18
The stone and brick walls are left untreated
Glasgow School of Art Library

TOP FLOOR

From the top of the stair eastwards runs a corridor rather grandly marked on the plans 'Loggia'. It has heavy brick arches more like a cellar beneath a building than a passageway on top. The three bay windows are equipped with folding tables where students still come for peace, or to draw the city's rooftops. Here too are the five staff studios. Moving east, the glazed passageway over the Museum roof, though labelled 'Pavilion' on the plans, has been known by generations of students as the Hen Run. It leads to the east section of the building, and to a large studio (now divided into two) which was once given over to Embroidery, an important activity in the School. At the extreme east end of the corridor a very low door gives on to the tower.

105
Bedford Lemere
LOGGIA, 1910
Photograph, negative no 20762/19
A printing press stands against the wall
Glasgow School of Art Library

106
LOGGIA
The brickwork has been painted white, losing
the warmth of the original scheme

BASEMENT ·

Placed within the insets of the E-shaped plan of the building, are two top-lit studios each with distinctive roof trusses. That to the east was the Anatomy studio. That to the west, with doors opening to roof height, was the Life Modelling Room. In this room the ends of the steel T-beams supporting the roof beams were split and forged into sculptural forms, a task which, it is said, brought the workmen out on strike.

At the west end is the Lecture Theatre with raked seating facing, unusually, into the corner of the room. Lecturers have their own entrance. The circular counter across the corner, useful for the display of objects, is in sections, and can be, and often was, removed for other dramatic presentations. Outside in the corridor, the walls of the adjacent studios allow, in their curves, for the provision of seating for those waiting for the Theatre to open.

The basement studios are lit by skylights in the area between the building and the street. Sculpture occupied the west studios, while in the east were housed ceramics, silversmithing, metalwork, enamelling, glass staining, woodcarving, and the special studio for drawing live animals. Between these were the fan room and the boiler house, to which coal was delivered through a chute in the pavement.

BOARD ROOM ·

The large studio immediately on the left of the entrance was turned into a materials store, an office, and a formal panelled Board Room also used by the School Secretary. The room is lit by three sets of nine lights each in circular beaten and pierced copper shades. A dozen new chairs for members of the Board were made each with three pierced crescent-like shapes in its back. Set into the wall, by the window, is Newbery's group portrait of the Building Committee. The dais on which the Chairman's chair was placed is still in this room. Along the east wall the panels conceal the doors of three large and useful presses. This dignified room has one unexpected feature, eight carved pilasters topped with Mackintosh's own free adaption of an egg and dart moulding set between two tiny Ionic volutes, the single reference in the School to classical architecture. It is easy to believe the story that this was intended as a poke in the eye for the establishment architects, who formed a significant section of the Board of Governors, as they sat at their meetings.

107
Bedford Lemere
WEST CORRIDOR, Basement, 1910
Photograph, negative no 20762/11
Few casts in this fine collection have survived
Glasgow School of Art Library

108
TWO COLUMNS
FROM THE NEW BOARD ROOM □ ■ ■
Next to the window the light creates a pattern of light on dark on the column, while in the interior of the room a dark on light pattern is created

109
Bedford Lemere
LIFE MODELLING STUDIO, 1910
Photograph, negative no 20762/12
The lighting system is clearly shown in this
basement sculpture studio
Glasgow School of Art Library

NOTES

1 A set of drawings dated June 1909 (Strathclyde Regional Council) does
   show the present front doors in position. This might show the intention,
   rather than the current situation.

2 John Summerson, *The Turn of the Century: Architecture in Britain around 1900*,
   University of Glasgow Press, 1976, p. 10, suggests that Shaw's New Zealand
   Chambers, Leadenhall Street, London (1872) with its asymmetrical
   entrance, inflected Mackintosh's design for the School. Mackintosh who
   read *The Studio* would probably have seen photographs of this in the well-
   illustrated article on Norman Shaw in vol. 7, 14 May 1896, p. 23.

3 Illustrated Roger Billcliffe, *Architectural Sketches & Flower Drawings by Charles
   Rennie Mackintosh*, Academy Editions, 1977, p. 32.

4 A selection of these appeared in the *British Architect*, vol. 44, 1895: 8 Nov.,
   pp. 332-3; 29 Nov., pp. 384-5, 388-9.

5 Illustrated *The Architect*, vol. 48, 22 July 1892, between pp. 56 & 57.

6 A clear drawing of the elevation in Frank Russell (ed.), *Art Nouveau
   Architecture*, Rizzoli, New York, 1979, p. 38. The doors also have affinities
   with the Art School doors.

7 David MacGibbon and Thomas Ross, *The Castellated and Domestic Architecture
   of Scotland*, vol. 2, 1887, p. 111; reprint, James Thin, 1971.

8 MacGibbon and Ross, *ibid*, vol. 3, 1889, p. 500.

9 Vol. 37, p. 210. See no. 76 in Joanna Symonds, *Catalogue of Drawings by
   C. F. A. Voysey in the Drawings Collection of the RIBA*, Gregg International, 1976.

10 MacGibbon & Ross, *ibid*, vol. 2, 1887, p. 280.

11 A possible source, not in the least direct, suggested for this façade is
   Charles Holden's Bristol Central Reference Library (1905-6).
   See Peter Davey, *Arts and Crafts Architecture*, Architectural Press, 1980,
   illustrated p. 124 with its Tudor-y 'broad mullioned flat, polygonal bays'.
   John Summerson, *ibid*, p. 24, notes 'The Tudor oriel theme in the art
   school is obvious enough; the remarkable thing is how un-Tudor it
   becomes in Mackintosh's hands'. For other suggested sources see
   Hiroaki Kimura, *Charles Rennie Mackintosh*, Process Architecture, Tokyo,
   1984, pp. 100, 102.

12 Reyner Banham, *Age of the Masters*, Architectural Press, 1975, p. 10.

13 In this Post-Freudian era, the subject can also be seen as an erect male
   organ.

14 Illustrated in *The Studio*, vol. 54, Oct. 1911, p. 39.

15 MacGibbon and Ross *ibid*, vol. 1, 1887, p. 206.

16 Roderick Gradidge, *Dream Houses: The Edwardian Ideal*, Constable, 1980,
   p. 163.

110
Maurice Greiffenhagen
FRA H. NEWBERY, 1913
Oil, 132.1 × 102.2 cm
Newbery stands at ease in front of the
School. Gifted to the Art Gallery by Newbery
in 1940
Glasgow Art Gallery & Museum

111
T & R Annan
VIEW FROM GLASGOW UNIVERSITY
TOWER, 1905
Photograph
Looking south-east to the Park Circus
Development of 1855, a fine example of the
city's planning and building
T & R Annan & Sons Ltd, Glasgow

REJECTING OVERT HISTORICISM
ARCHITECTURAL INFLUENCES

JAMES MACAULAY

THROUGHOUT Mackintosh's professional career Glasgow was not only Britain's Second City, as it had been during most of the nineteenth century, but by the 1890s it had become Europe's sixth largest city taking its place immediately after the imperial capitals of Berlin, Vienna and St Petersburg. In 1801 the population of Glasgow was 77,000; by the mid-century it had reached almost half a million; and by the opening of the twentieth century that figure had doubled. Although much of the city's wealth and reputation was based on heavy industries, with the Clyde producing one-third of the total British shipping tonnage by 1880, it was claimed that there was almost no product which was not manufactured within the area encompassed by greater Glasgow.[1]

To accommodate the astonishing increase in population and manufacturing and industrial capacity the city's boundaries were continuously being pushed outwards. Its medieval origins and its importance as an entrepôt in the Georgian period were so overlaid in the Victorian age that Glasgow, even in the 1960s, could still be described as 'the finest surviving example of a great Victorian city.'[2]

Yet, when Mackintosh was born in 1868, the largest single building was still the medieval cathedral though it would soon be overtaken by Sir George Gilbert Scott's new university buildings on Gilmorehill, in which English and Flemish Gothic were mingled with Scottish traits, and by William Young's City Chambers, an untidy conglomerate of Renaissance idioms. Despite such extremes of architectural

taste, much of the centre of Glasgow was stylistically conservative. The overall scale was dictated by the fact that Glasgow was and always has been, at least until the present decades, a stone city. For centuries local quarries had provided varieties of cream- and honey-coloured sandstones and when these dried up red sandstone was imported by sea and by rail from the island of Arran, north Ayrshire and Dumfriesshire. The sandstones were soft enough to allow for much ornamental work whether it was the huge overmuscled Atlantes on the portal of J. T. Rochead's St Vincent Street Bank of Scotland (1869), one of the handsomest of the palazzi in the commercial quarter, or a well-lettered datestone on one of the terraces in the west end. Undoubtedly, stone gives the city a scale and a grandeur unmatched by any provincial, brick-built and stucco-clad English city so that architecturally one has to compare Glasgow with continental counterparts such as Milan and Vienna. After all, where else in Britain can one find such limitless cliffs of stone as line West Princes Street or edge Great Western Road?

The tradition of stone working was matched by a strong classical inspiration. Glasgow's architects were a close-knit community albeit fiercely jealous and often bitter about one another's failings. Although Robert Adam had been called in at the close of the eighteenth century to provide for the new need for such public buildings as the Royal Infirmary and Assembly Rooms and though early residential developments in the fashionable west end imitated what was happening in Edinburgh's New Town, on the whole what was required in Glasgow was provided by Glasgow men. Robert Adam's concept of classical grandeur was enlarged by David Hamilton with his lavish Graeco-Romano Royal Exchange (1827) with its gigantic octastyle portico which was the subject of a premiated measured drawing by Mackintosh.[3] As the century progressed the undiluted purities of the Greek Revival came to be preferred. A severe example is the former Elgin Place Congregational Church in Bath Street (1856), by John Burnet senior, where the temple form was enhanced by a high podium and a hexastyle portico displaying the dry eclecticism of Greek scholarship. The dominant architectu-

112
VIEW OVER THE ROOF OF THE ART SCHOOL
The ventilators protrude from the School's flat roof. This view, from the east tower looking west, has the spire of Glasgow University on the skyline

113
George Gilbert Scott
DESIGN FOR GLASGOW UNIVERSITY, n d
From C. A. Oakley, 'The Second City', 1967, p. 150
The balustrades were omitted and the spire was redesigned by Scott's son, John Oldrid
Glasgow School of Art Library

Alexander Thomson
ST VINCENT STREET CHURCH, 1858 □■
Photograph by T & R Annan
The podium contains the church while the
temple contains the galleries and top of the
main hall. The lettering on the shop front in
the foreground is in suitable style
T & R Annan & Sons Ltd, Glasgow

114
David Hamilton
ROYAL EXCHANGE, GLASGOW, 1827
Print by Joseph Swan
John M. Leighton, *Strath Clutha or the
Beauties of Clyde*, 1838(39?) opposite p. 50
In 1887 Mackintosh won second prize from
the Glasgow Institute of Architects for his
measured drawings of the Royal Exchange
James W. Murray

ral influence, however, was Alexander ('Greek') Thomson in whose memory, after his death in 1875, a student travelling scholarship was established. The set subject in 1890 was a public hall, in 'the Early Classic style', to seat 1000 persons. In Mackintosh's winning scheme not only did he select the Ionic order, Thomson's preferred order, but he composed his elevations with numerous Thomson idioms as used by James Sellars in the St Andrew's Halls.[4]

Thomson's series of bizarre churches is portrayed in all the architectural textbooks. Of his three important churches only the St Vincent Street Church (1858) survives intact on a steeply sloping south-facing hill (characteristic of many Glasgow sites including the School of Art). Thomson

attempted to follow the tenets of orthodox Greek classicism without reference to later architectural epochs. Thus, in a public lecture he castigated Roman architecture because 'the adoption of the arch by the Romans had strewed Europe with ruins'.[5] Nevertheless, such narrow extremism cannot detract from the inventive unorthodoxy of the St Vincent Street Church where Thomson had to accommodate the worshippers (tickets were required for the opening service) within the limitations imposed by the auditory nature of presbyterian services so that the temple form is compromised by the insertion of side aisles and galleries while the most striking innovation is the detached tower set to one side like a Lombardic campanile. The structure of the church is interesting technically because of Thomson's use of iron load-bearing columns, of plate glass, which is glazed directly to the stonework, and the brilliant paint colouring perhaps inspired by the recent publication of *The Grammar of Ornament* (1856) by Owen Jones. After Thomson's death his influence continued with James Sellars whose St Andrew's Halls (1873), built at a cost of £100,000, uses many of Thomson's idioms within a framework borrowed from Schinkel's Altes Museum in Berlin. The strength of this classical strain can still be seen in Hugh Barclay's St George's-in-the-Fields (1886) though it was losing its vigour when it came to the Langside Hill Church (1895) by Alexander Skirving, Thomson's former draughtsman.

In a technically inventive city such as Glasgow it would have been surprising if the architects had not responded to the opportunities presented by the developing iron technology. Thus, the city centre has much pioneering ferro-vitreous construction. John Baird I (the mentor of Thomson) was the designer of the Argyle Arcade (1827), where hammer-beams carry exposed iron and glass top-lighting, and of Gardner's warehouse in Jamaica Street (1855) which has an exposed cast-iron frame. Just as impressive is John Honeyman's Ca d'Oro in Union Street (1872) where, despite the outward stylistic difference between it and Gardner's, the same rational structuralism permits maximum light to penetrate the deep display areas.

116
John Baird I
ARGYLE ARCADE, 1827 □■
An early example in Glasgow of ferro-vitreous construction

117
John Honeyman
LANSDOWNE CHURCH, Great Western Road,
1862
Photograph by T & R Annan
A skilful and original interpretation of Early
English Gothic

T & R Annan & Sons Ltd, Glasgow

In the history of the city and of Mackintosh, John Honeyman has an important place. Originally destined for the ministry, he became an architect and, possibly because of his church connections, secured numerous ecclesiastical commissions for his firm including perhaps the Queen's Cross Church (1898) for which the drawings were prepared by Mackintosh then still a draughtsman in Honeyman & Keppie. Honeyman's most original ecclesiastical design must be Lansdowne Church, Great Western Road (1862), which, though expressing correct Early English Gothic, displays freedom in composition as well as ingenious planning. Honeyman was notable as a restorer. Having worked on the medieval cathedral, he contributed a scholarly chapter to *The Book of Glasgow Cathedral* (1898) and in 1902, when the School of Art was half built, John Honeyman and John Keppie were completing the restoration of Brechin Cathedral where no trace of the waywardness of the art nouveau touches the thoughtful scholarship overlying the medieval work.

118
Photographer Unknown
JOHN HONEYMAN
From George Eyre-Todd *Who's Who in Glasgow in 1909*, Gowans & Gray, 1909, p. 91
The 'scholarly and dignified' founder of the firm of Honeyman, Keppie & Mackintosh. In 1889 John Keppie became a partner; Mackintosh, in 1901
Glasgow School of Art Library

119
GLASGOW CATHEDRAL, Section,
East End
From MacGibbon & Ross, *The Ecclesiastical
Architecture of Scotland*, vol 2, 1896, p. 185
The principles of rational structuralism in
Gothic architecture as expounded by Pugin
are also demonstrated in Mackintosh's work
Glasgow School of Art Library

Glasgow Cathedral must have been the earliest piece of architecture which Mackintosh would have encountered. Set below a hill, immediately to the west of Dennistoun where Mackintosh was brought up, its strong clean outline must have appealed to the artist in Mackintosh who, in 1890, produced a watercolour of the eastern silhouette against the sunset. For the architect what was appealing about the cathedral was the double-storeyed east end (unique in Britain) made necessary by the sloping site and the engineering problems that had been solved in raising a structure 140 ft high. Indeed, a cross-section of the east end has some affinities with the section of Mackintosh's west wing in the School of Art. Internally, the control of the spatial volumes in the cathedral and their inter-connections at the crossing must have provided Mackintosh with thought as they still do for any intelligent architect today. Indeed, it may be that the forms and planning of Glasgow Cathedral provided the starting point for Mackintosh's entry for the Liverpool Cathedral competition in 1903.

Glasgow Cathedral, dating mostly from the thirteenth and fourteenth centuries, is in that style of unornamented Gothic which most appealed to A. W. N. Pugin. Because Mackintosh is hailed as a pioneer of modernism it is all too easy to overlook the fact that he was a Victorian and that his architectural teaching would have been based on the precepts of Pugin and of Ruskin who, it is claimed, was one of Mackintosh's favourite authors[6] although that did not prevent him from lecturing on the failings, as he saw them, of *The Stones of Venice*.[7] Glasgow Cathedral, with its visible structural logic and lack of decoration, accorded with Pugin's most famous precept that, 'The two great rules for design are these: 1st, that there should be no features about a building which are not necessary for convenience, construction or propriety; 2nd, that all ornament should consist of the essential construction of the building.'[8] The architecture of his own time was condemned by Pugin. 'Architectural features are continually tacked on buildings with which they have no connexion, merely for the sake of what is termed effect.' What Pugin sought was 'the decoration of construction'[9] although

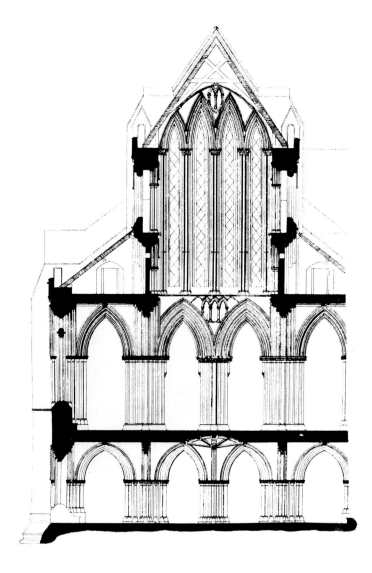

120
Charles R. Mackintosh
GLASGOW CATHEDRAL AT SUNSET, 1890
Watercolour, 39.4 × 28.3 cm
Painted while Mackintosh lived at 2 Firpark
Terrace, near the Cathedral
*Hunterian Art Gallery, University of Glasgow,
Mackintosh Collection*

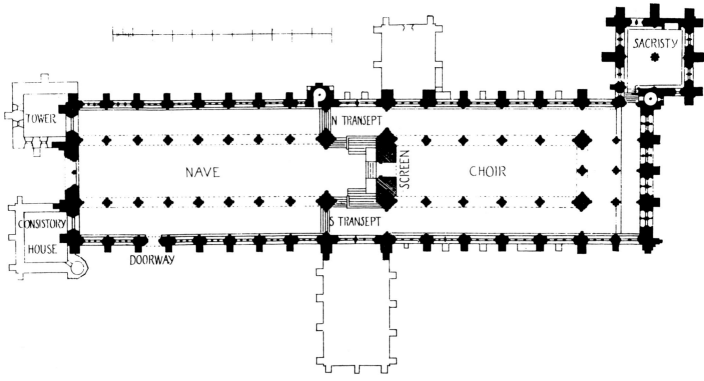

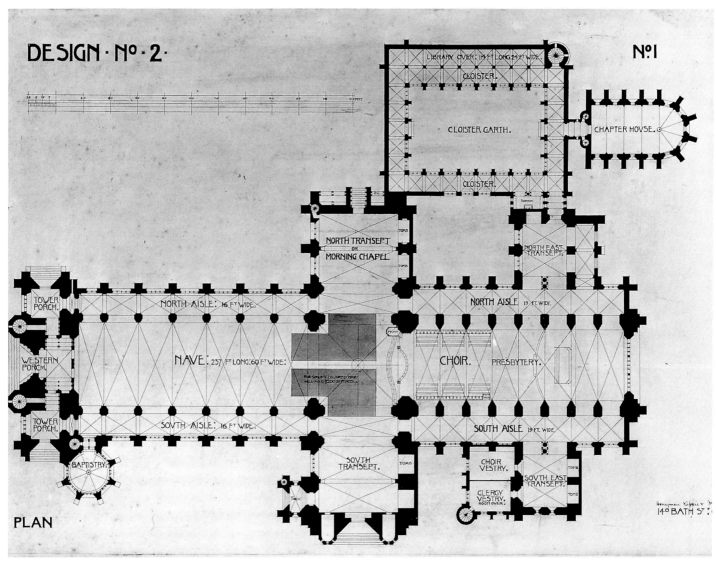

DESIGN · Nº · 2 ·   Nº I

PLAN

he was sufficiently a child of his own time to require that, 'An architect should exhibit his skill by turning the difficulties which occur in raising an elevation from a convenient plan into so many picturesque beauties.'[10] From Ruskin Mackintosh would have learnt: 'Never encourage imitation or copying of any kind.'[11] In Gothic architecture what Ruskin found most appealing was 'naturalism and changefulness' so that, 'Whenever it finds occasion for change in its form or purpose, it submits to it without the slightest sense of loss either to its unity or majesty' and he considered further that, 'It is one of the chief virtues of the Gothic builders, that they never suffered ideas of outside symmetries and consistencies to interfere with the real use and value of what they did'.[12]

Anyone looking at the Glasgow School of Art can see how closely Mackintosh followed these precepts. Of course, Pugin's and Ruskin's search for a national English style of architecture did not, strictly speaking, apply in Scotland where the historical tradition found its finest expression in the native castles and tower-houses. It was that tradition which was apostrophised by Mackintosh in a paper on Scottish Baronial architecture delivered to the Glasgow Architectural Association in 1891. 'In the castles of the 15th century . . . every feature was useful. In the 16th century also, however exaggerated some of the corbels and other features might be they are still distinguished from the later examples of the 17th century by their genuineness and utility.' He praised the planning also as the generator of architectural form[13] and in doing so dissociated himself from the school of nineteenth-century Scots-Baronialism which had been engendered by William Burn and David Bryce.

Mackintosh's interest in Scotland's past would have been fostered by the appearance of *The Castellated and Domestic Architecture of Scotland* by David MacGibbon and Thomas Ross, which in five volumes published between 1887 and 1892, presented a chronological review and analysis of the country's stock of castellated buildings. More importantly, from Mackintosh's point of view, the authors provided for the first time plans, sections and elevation as well as details of every structure. These could supplement, where need be, Mackintosh's own sketches of Maybole Castle, Ayrshire, which would re-emerge in the east gable of the School of Art, or of Falkland Palace which would be regenerated as the Scotland Street School. The availability of MacGibbon and Ross's work as an architectural primer coincided with the publication in 1892 of W. R. Lethaby's *Architecture, Mysticism and Myth* which reinforced Mackintosh's belief in the timeless worth of indigenous buildings since, 'Old architecture lived because it had purpose. Modern architecture to be real must not be an envelope without contents.'[14]

By the closing decades of the century architectural concepts were being disseminated rapidly and nationally with the rise of the architectural magazines such as *The Builder* (the oldest), *Architectural Review* and *The British Architect*, which featured projects by Honeyman & Keppie including many drawn by Mackintosh. Then in 1893 came *The Studio* which drew attention to the designs of C. F. A. Voysey who, according to Francis Newbery, was the young Mackintosh's chief inspiration.[15] Voysey's idiomatic white roughcast walls, exaggerated verticals, overriding catslide roofs and elevations sculpted in simple masses accorded with Mackintosh's interest in the Scottish building tradition while rejecting overt historicism. The appealing freshness and vigour of Voysey's architecture, in which he sought to 'eschew all imitation'[16], is evident in his published design for studios in Chelsea (1892) where the expansive lights with only the slimmest of divisions compare with what would soon appear on the north elevation of the Glasgow School of Art. Yet, since Voysey's output was mostly domestic, Mackintosh had to look elsewhere when designing a large public building and turned most successfully to Norman Shaw whose use of stacked window grids beneath gabled heads, derived ultimately from Pugin's Bilston Grange (1841), as used at Leyswood (1867) and Adcote (1876), were replicated in the west wing of the School of Art. Shaw's New Zealand Chambers (1872) must surely also have been studied by Mackintosh, either consciously or as a memory, when composing the entrance to the School of Art although references

can also be made to the Mary Ward Settlement, London (1892), and to the Ladbroke Grove Library, London (1890). Nearer home an innovative work was James MacLaren's Stirling High School (1887) extension (1888) where the observatory tower and new wing with simple massing and uncluttered verticality predate by only a few years the east elevation of the School of Art. Nevertheless, the portions and fragments of these and of other buildings, contemporary and historical, are only the genes of the Glasgow School of Art. Its fame, as one of the pioneering achievements of the

Modern Movement, is because in his planning, spatial control and elevational composition Mackintosh accepted the premise of Voysey, when praising Gothic architecture, that 'outside appearances are evolved from internal fundamental conditions; staircases and windows come from where most convenient for use. All openings are proportioned to the various parts to which they apply.'[17] It was from the theory and antecedents of the nineteenth century that Mackintosh evolved a work which sounded a clarion call for a new age.

NOTES

[1]   Charles Oakley, *'The Second City'*, Blackie, 1967, pp. 31, 70, 74, 113.

[2]   Lord Esher, *Conservation in Glasgow: A Preliminary Report*, Corporation of Glasgow, 1971, p. 1.

[3]   Thomas Howarth, *Charles Rennie Mackintosh and the Modern Movement*, Routledge & Kegan Paul, 2nd edn., 1977, p. 5.

[4]   *Ibid*, pp. 7-9; Ronald McFadzean, *The Life and Work of Alexander Thomson*, Routledge & Kegan Paul, 1979, pp. 273-4. For an analysis of Mackintosh's early designs and use of architectural sources see David M. Walker, 'The Early Work of Charles Rennie Mackintosh', in Nikolaus Pevsner and J. M. Richards (eds.), *The Anti-Rationalists*, Architectural Press, 1973, pp. 116-35.

[5]   Alexander Thomson, 'Art and Architecture', *The British Architect*, 1874, Lecture IV, p. 8.

[6]   Howarth, *op. cit.*, p. 7.

[7]   Charles Rennie Mackintosh, 'Criticism of Ruskin's *Stones of Venice*', F(g), Hunterian Art Gallery, University of Glasgow, Mackintosh Collection.

[8]   A. W. N. Pugin, *True Principles of Pointed or Christian Architecture*, Academy Editions, 1973, p. 1.

[9]   *Ibid*.

[10]   *Ibid*, p. 72.

[11]   John Ruskin, *Stones of Venice*, George Allen, 1904, vol. II, p. 197.

[12]   *Ibid*, vol II, p. 212.

[13]   Charles Rennie Mackintosh, 'Scotch Baronial Architecture', F(c), Hunterian Art Gallery, University of Glasgow, Mackintosh Collection.

[14]   Charles Rennie Mackintosh, 'Architecture', Hunterian Art Gallery, University of Glasgow, Mackintosh Collection, F(h).

[15]   Alastair Service (ed.), *Edwardian Architecture and Its Origins*, Architectural Press, 1975, p. 155.

[16]   *Ibid*, p. 121.

[17]   C. F. A. Voysey, 'The English Home', *The British Architect*, vol. 75, 1911, p. 60.

GLASGOW ART
GLASGOW CRAFT
GLASGOW INTERNATIONAL

WILLIAM
BUCHANAN

Nowhere has the modern movement of art been entered upon more seriously than at Glasgow; the church, the school, the house, the restaurant, the shop, the poster, the book, with its printing, illustration and binding, have all come under the spell of the new influence. (THE STUDIO, vol. 38, 1907, pp. 31-2.)

It is now Glasgow rather than London which is likely to give modern art its new direction. (P. Forthuny, 'L'Art Décoratif en Ecosse', REVUE DES ARTS DÉCORATIFS, vol. 22, 1902, p. 61.)

AT the turn of the century Glasgow was the centre of a huge soot-grimed apparatus which turned coal and ore first into iron and steel and then into ships, locomotives, bridges, pumps, hydraulic presses, cranes, and machinery for cotton, jute, and sugar mills. These it supplied to the world. Above all, there was a very special understanding with the steam engine; Glasgow bred men who found satisfaction in its logic, and beauty in its smooth and efficient running. The work force, labouring under paternalistic employers, took great pride in its skills. Some Glaswegians lived in the most appalling slums, most lived in tenements, terraces, and a few in handsome villas.

William Burrell and his brother made a fortune not only from their shipping line which traded with India, China, Japan, Australia, the Baltic and the United States, but also from the shrewd buying and selling of ships. Burrell was to leave his great art collection, which includes superb medieval tapestries, to the city. Glasgow, through its great labour, became prosperous and proud.

Patrons of the Arts appeared. A great surge of creative energy spilled into painting, architecture, embroidery, metalwork, graphic design and photography. The first impetus came in the early 1880s with the appearance of the Glasgow Boys. The Boys, who disliked being called a School, were a group of painters dissatisfied with the sentimental, anecdotal painting of their time and angry with the Royal Scottish Academy for not exhibiting their work. If Mackintosh read the November 1889 issue of the Boys' *Scottish Art Review* he would recognise, in an attack against the Academy, that their problem had been the same as his own. A young artist realises why his work is not acceptable. 'I had been painting nature as I saw it. In future if I would become an Academician, I must paint nature as the Academy saw it.' The Boys showed that worn-out credos could be overthrown. In their case, the establishment eventually conceded by electing them to membership. James Guthrie, indeed, was to become President of the Academy in 1902 and was knighted the next year.

Mackintosh would certainly have been aware of the second phase of the Boys' development when some of them abandoned tonal, *plein-air,* painting and, under influences which included Japanese art, their work took on a more decorative aspect. One of the key pictures is George Henry's *A Galloway Landscape* (Glasgow Art Gallery). Surely Mackintosh would have responded to its powerful evocation of autumn when it was shown in 1890 in the Glasgow Institute of the Fine Arts' galleries (designed in 1878 by J. J. Burnet back from his Beaux-Arts training in Paris)? That exhibition also contained work by Honeyman & Keppie, the firm for which he now worked. They exhibited *The Principal Entrance of New Offices for the Fairfield Shipbuilding and Engineering Co. Ltd.* Keppie himself showed a painting, *Street Scene in Chartres.* By 1895 Mackintosh was not only showing at the Institute but designing its poster as well. In the exhibition that year his *Design for Diploma, Glasgow School of Art Club* and *A Railway Terminus — Longitudinal Section* were hung in the company of some of the Boys: Crawhall's *Rabbit,* Lavery's *Croquet,* Guthrie's *Midsummer,* and Hornel's *A Geisha.* Honeyman & Keppie showed *Queen Margaret College Medical Department,* though this may have been a study drawn by Mackintosh. J. J. Burnet exhibited his *New Pathological Building, Western Infirmary.*

In 1895 E. A. Hornel held an exhibition of paintings, the result of his trip to Japan with George Henry in 1893-4. This must have been visited by Mackintosh because he was deeply interested in things Japanese. Mackintosh would

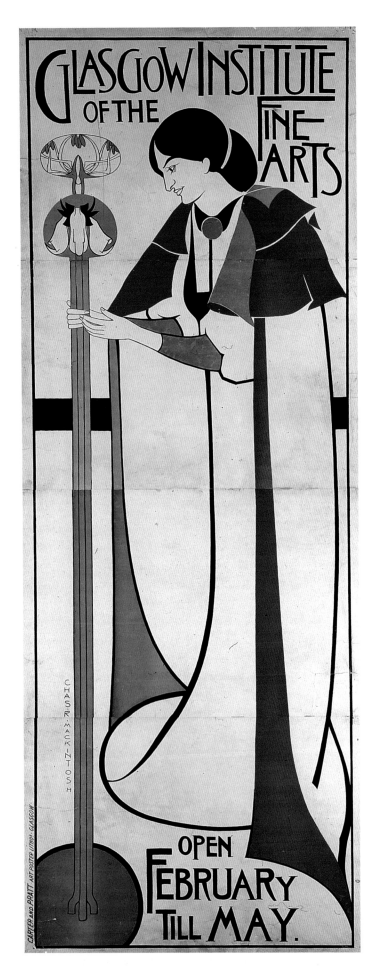

124
Charles R. Mackintosh
POSTER FOR THE GLASGOW INSTITUTE
OF THE FINE ARTS, 1895
Lithograph, 223.8 × 89 cm
The forms in the circular motif above the
woman's hand relate closely to the drawing of
a foxglove made in Corrie

Hunterian Art Gallery, University of Glasgow, Mackintosh
Collection

125
Artist unknown
IN THE HAUNTS OF ART, 1895
A caricature of Mackintosh's Institute poster
appears in the top right-hand corner. This
accompanied an account of the Institute's
opening in the *Evening Times,* 5 Feb. 1895,
which noted that 'The Misses Macdonald in
sacque gowns and muslin fichus were most
aesthetic'

Glasgow Room, Mitchell Library

have met the Boys themselves in the Art Club at 185 Bath Street when, in 1892, working with Keppie, the firm remodelled the premises and added a large gallery. Mackintosh never became a member; Keppie eventually became a fixture.

The crafts received a powerful charge from the arrival of Francis Newbery at the School of Art in 1885. Doubtless Newbery had a large hand in bringing the second exhibition of the Arts and Crafts Exhibition Society from London to the Corporation Galleries. This included fabrics by Voysey, friezes by Crane, a box and a bookplate by Lethaby, a hanging electrolier by Belcher, and carpets and printed textiles by Morris & Co. A direct result of this must have been the setting up in the School, two years later, of studios for Stained Glass, Needlework, Pottery, Metalwork and Bookbinding. As the Arts and Crafts exhibition opened on 18 January 1890 there would have been time for Walter Crane's decorative gesso panels to impinge on George Henry and E. A. Hornel as they worked on their joint painting *The Druids* (Glasgow Art Gallery). This, completed by the end of March, also made use of gesso and has a decided decorative quality.

Several Arts and Crafts luminaries came to the School to speak: in 1888 Walter Crane, in 1889 William Morris, and in 1890 Lewis F. Day. But the break with the Arts and Crafts movement happened in 1896 after the work of Mackintosh, MacNair and the Macdonald sisters was seen and decidedly not liked in London. *The Studio* magazine publicised Glasgow work and stimulated artists in Glasgow as it did everywhere else.

The development of embroidery was driven forward by Newbery's wife, Jessie Rowat, whose course began in 1894. This was continued by Ann Macbeth who took over in 1908. Embroidery found its way on to clothes which were also specially designed. Dresses for children by Jessie Newbery were illustrated in the periodical *Moderne Stickerein* (published by Alex Koch in Darmstadt between 1903 and 1909). This interest in dress design and embroidery was shared with Anna Muthesius[1] who used photographs of Margaret and Frances Macdonald and both Newbery daughters in her book about dress *Das Eigenkleid der Frau* (published in 1903 by Kramer & Baum in Krefeld). Frances Macdonald designed the cover.

Anna Muthesius and her husband were close friends of the Newberys and the Mackintoshes. Hermann Muthesius understood the Mackintoshes' work and championed it through his article in *Dekorative Kunst* in March 1902, and in *Das englische Haus* published in three volumes by Wasmuth, Berlin, from 1904, although the loosely applied title of the latter publication may have made Mackintosh wince a little.

The graphic work of Jessie M. King became well known. Her finest work may be her illustrations for *The*

126
Heywood Sumner
INSIGNIA OF THE ARTS AND CRAFTS
EXHIBITION SOCIETY, 1888
A tortured attempt to show the integration of the arts, crafts, and architecture, from the tailpiece in the exhibition catalogue of 1889
Glasgow Museums & Art Galleries

127
J. Craig Annan
ANN MACBETH, n d
Photograph
Her detachable collar, worked with Glasgow
Style rose and leaf motif, is illustrated in *The
Studio,* vol 44, 1908, p. 291
Glasgow Museums & Art Galleries

128
Jessie Rowat Newbery
CUSHION COVER, n d
Natural linen with brown and green linen
appliqué, embroidered with pale blue and
green thread, 56.1 × 47.2 cm
   Time passeth and I speaketh not
   Deth cometh and I warneth not
   Amend today and slack not
   Tomorrow thyself cannot
National Museums of Scotland

Defence of Guenevere and other Poems by William Morris
in the edition published by The Bodley Head in 1904. 'A
haunting and tender evocation of a fragile medieval dream-
world such as that conjured up by Maeterlinck's early plays.'[2]
She also made jewellery and produced textile designs for,
like most Glasgow designers, she could turn her hand to
more than one craft.

   It was not by mere chance that such a strong group of
women appeared, but as a result of the policy of the School.
The Chairman at the annual meeting in 1885 stated: 'I
believe that, in the Fine Arts, women . . . will take a distinguished place, as has been done by many, such as
Rosa Bonheur, Elizabeth Thompson, Clara Montalba, Alice
Havers, and others, and will, I trust, [be taken] by many of
our Lady Students here.'

   In addition to these designers and craft workers a
group of women painters emerged. They included Norah
Neilson Gray, Stansmore Dean Stevenson and Bessie Mac-
Nicol. The Glasgow Society of Lady Artists was formed in
1882. Later Club was added to this title. In 1895 they held a
Fancy Fair in the Institute Galleries to raise funds for the purchase of their own premises. Mackintosh, it is said, tapped
the stick for the curtains to open for the *tableaux vivants*
which included *La Belle Dame Sans Merci.* The Club was
able to buy, in the next year, 5 Blythswood Square. They
asked George Walton to decorate it, which he did in pale
green, and in the new picture gallery (designed by Fred
Rowntree) he built a huge stone fireplace and provided hood,
backplate and firedogs. Mackintosh was asked to re-
decorate the Club house in 1908. This generated a 'brisk
little storm'[3] and resulted in Mackintosh's black door in the
otherwise formal Square today.

129
George Henry and E. A. Hornel
THE DRUIDS — BRINGING IN THE
MISTLETOE, 1890
Oil, 152.4 × 152.4 cm
This joint painting marks a change to
decorative concerns after the earlier tonal
painting of the Glasgow Boys
Glasgow Museums & Art Galleries

130
Mihya-Diez Dührkoop
ELSIE NEWBERY IN BERLIN, c. 1913
Photographed in the home of the Muthesius
family wearing a dress designed by Anna
Muthesius
Eckart Muthesius

131
J. Craig Annan
ANNA MUTHESIUS, c. 1902
Photogravure 20.6 × 15.5 cm
from *Camera Work* Oct. 1904
Anna Muthesius (nee Trippenbach) gave up her career as a singer on her marriage to Hermann Muthesius. He consulted her on colour, furniture and interior design
University of Exeter Library

132
Jessie M. King
OF MARGARET SITTING GLORIOUS THERE
Illustration to 'The Eve of Crécy' from William Morris, *The Defence of Guenevere and other Poems*, published by John Lane, 1904, p. 219
　　Of Margaret sitting glorious there,
　　In glory of gold and glory of hair,
　　And glory of glorious face most fair; —
　　Ah! qu'elle est belle, La Marguerite.
Glasgow School of Art Library

133
Jessie M. King
COVER OF *The Defence of Guenevere and other Poems*
By William Morris, published by John Lane, 1904
Glasgow School of Art Library

·OF·MARGARET·SITTING·GLORIOUS·THERE·

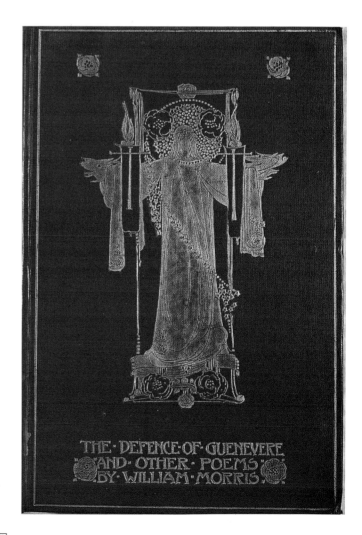

134
Charles R. Mackintosh
■□ THE HARVEST MOON, 1892
Watercolour, 35.2 × 27.7 cm
An inscription on the back records its gift by
Mackintosh to Keppie in October 1894
Glasgow School of Art

136
Margaret and Frances Macdonald
FRAME, 1897 □■□
Beaten aluminium, 69 × 60.5 cm
Annan paid five guineas for this frame in
which he exhibited *Molly*, a portrait of a child,
at the London Photographic Salon in 1897
Private Collection

137
Margaret and Frances Macdonald
CLOCK FACE, c. 1896 □□■
Brass, 52.1 × 48 cm
The clock complete with its stand is
reproduced in *The Studio*, vol 11, 1897, p. 95
Present location unknown

135
Bessie MacNicol
A GIRL OF THE 'SIXTIES', c. 1900
Oil, 81 × 60.7 cm
Shown at the International Society Exhibition
in London in 1901. Once in the collection of
John Keppie
Glasgow Museums & Art Galleries

That photography could be art of the highest calibre
was demonstrated in 1892 by James Craig Annan when he
exhibited his fresh and vital photographs, then dismissed as
'modern eccentricities',[4] taken on a tour in the north of Hol-
land. His tiny *The Beach at Zandvoort* was published in *The
Studio* in London in 1894, and in both the *Photographic

Times, New York, and the *Photographische Blätter*, Vienna,
the following year. In 1899 it appeared in *Photographische
Centralblatt* from Munich. It must have been seen by almost
anyone seriously interested in photography then. Annan
obtained, perhaps commissioned, in 1897 a frame in beaten
aluminium for his photograph *Molly* from Frances and
Margaret Macdonald at their workshop at 123 Hope Street.
About that time he also acquired a clock by them for his
dining room. It is to be wondered if he understood the significance of the shapes made between the pairs of hands
and arms of the two figures on either side of the dial. Do they
signal, in a startlingly frank way, consciously or not, the
blossoming relationship between the sisters and Mackintosh
and MacNair?

J. Taylor, writing in *The Studio* in 1907[5], showed just
how seriously interior design was taken in Glasgow, 'with
some recent schemes of decoration [the artist] has indicated
the design and colour of the gowns to be worn, so that no disturbing element might mar the unity of the conception'. The
Glasgow designer George Walton, setting up in London, was
probably introduced by Annan to George Davison, photographer and European manager of Kodak. Davison commissioned Walton to design the Kodak showrooms. A new style
would promote a new art. Those who walked in to Leipziger-
strasse 114, Berlin, or any of the other Kodak shops in Brussels, Moscow, St Petersburg, London, Milan, Glasgow, Dublin
or Vienna walked straight into the Glasgow Style. As the
Amateur Photographer said, 'One could fancy persons of
an aesthetic temperament taking up "Kodakraphy" through
sheer sympathy with its Glasgow habitat.'[6] One of Davison's
homes, and his houseboat, both designed by Walton,
appear in Annan's *The White House*. This photograph, like

138
George Walton
KODAK SHOWROOM, BRUSSELS □■
At 59 Montagne de la Cour. An illustration to
the article by Hermann Muthesius, 'Die
Kodak-Läden George Walton', *Dekorative
Kunst*, March 1903, pp. 210-21
Glasgow School of Art Library

139
J. Craig Annan
THE WHITE HOUSE, 1909
Photogravure, 19.6 × 17.4 cm
Both the White House and the houseboat
were designed by George Walton for George
Davison of Kodak

Scottish National Portrait Gallery, Edinburgh

140
J. Craig Annan
CHARLES R. MACKINTOSH, 1893 □ ■
Photograph
Mackintosh, every bit the turn-of-the-century
dandy, not only cultivates a tiny curl on his
forehead but discards a waistcoat and sports
a large bow tie with a loose collar. His partner
Keppie was bearded and wore stiff stand-up
collars

Glasgow School of Art Library

Mackintosh's School of Art, has an important place in the history of its medium. It is recognised as one of the 'seminal examples of the instantaneous snapshot wedded by vision into the formal concerns of modern art'.[7]

J. Craig Annan photographed most of these Glasgow artists. He produced in 1908 a large volume *The Glasgow School of Painters* with an introduction by Baldwin Brown, published by Maclehose in Glasgow and complete with portraits of each artist and reproductions of their work in photogravure of which he was an acknowledged master. It is Annan's portrait of Mackintosh — 'Toshy' to his friends — with floppy bow tie, soft moustache and tiny curl at forehead which has become the icon of the man. The family firm of T. & R. Annan recorded many of Mackintosh's interiors.

International exhibitions were powerful stimuli then. Glasgow had such a successful one in 1888 that its profits were applied to the building of a new municipal art gallery. A second international exhibition was held in 1901 to celebrate the gallery's opening. The latter exhibition was for which Mackintosh designed his circular concert hall, part of his unsuccessful submission for the exhibition competition. In 1902 the International Exhibition of Modern Decorative Art in Turin displayed a sample of what was being created in Glasgow. Annan won a medal in the photography section. As well as an interior by Mackintosh and Margaret Macdonald Mackintosh, and one by Frances Macdonald MacNair and Herbert MacNair, there were, among others, embroidery by Jessie Newbery and Ann Macbeth, and furniture by E. A. Taylor, husband of Jessie M. King who won a gold medal for her book cover for *L'Evangile de L'Enfance*.[8]

Work from Glasgow had an influence both on the Continent of Europe and in the United States. The Boys exhibited regularly in Munich from 1890 and helped to bring about the Secession of Munich artists. At the first exhibition of the Vienna Secession in 1898 two of them, John Lavery and E. A. Walton, were invited to participate. At the fourth exhibition, in 1899, work by ten Glasgow Boys and one Glasgow Girl, Bessie MacNicol, was on view. Perhaps they paved the way for Mackintosh, MacNair, and Frances and Margaret Macdonald to show at the eighth exhibition in 1900? Mackintosh and his group, and the Boys, were seen, separately, elsewhere in Europe. Exhibitions of the Boys' work toured in the United States in 1895, 1896, and 1905. Annan contributed to most of the important European photographic exhibitions and his work was seen in Philadelphia in 1894, in New York in 1905 and in Buffalo in 1910 as well as being reproduced in the influential American publication *Camera Work*.

Mackintosh was part of a group of outward-looking artists whose reputations went far beyond Britain, let alone Scotland. He worked in an exciting city which generated new ideas in both science and the visual arts. His prodigious talents enabled him to paint, to design, and to build. His art is the supreme manifestation of Glasgow's artistic creativity.

NOTES

[1] See also Isobel Spencer, 'Francis Newbery and the Glasgow Style', *Apollo*, Oct. 1973, p. 293.

[2] John Russell Taylor, *The Art Nouveau Book in Britain*, Methuen, 1966, p. 132.

[3] DeCourcy Lewthwaite Dewar, *History of the Glasgow Society of Lady Artists' Club*, privately printed, Maclehose, 1950, p. 22. See also Ailsa Tanner, *Glasgow Society of Lady Artists*, Catalogue, Glasgow Society of Women Artists, 1982.

[4] *American Amateur Photographer*, July 1896, p. 298.

[5] J. Taylor, 'Modern Decorative Art at Glasgow', *The Studio*, vol. 38, pp. 31-2.

[6] *Amateur Photographer*, vol. 32, 1900, p. 156.

[7] Jonathan Green, *Camera Work: A Critical Anthology*, Aperture, New York, 1973, p. 22.

[8] *L'Evangile de l'Enfance de N. S. J(esus) C)hrist selon St Pierre d'après le manuscrit de l'Abbaye de St Wolfgang*, Paris, n.d. It was rebound by Maclehose in Glasgow for the Turin exhibition. Its frontispiece is illustrated in *The Studio*, vol. 26, 1902, p. 185.

THE MACKINTOSH INHERITANCE

PETER TROWLES

WHILE the Glasgow School of Art is undoubtedly Mackintosh's supreme architectural achievement, the building, which continues as a lively educational institution, now fulfils two new and equally important roles: that of a working museum dedicated to Mackintosh and that of a reference and resource centre for the academic study of the man and his art. The building and its interior continues to attract the attention of academics, scholars, architects and designers throughout the world.

In recent years, however, and most noticeably since the early 1980s, the School's Collection has been the centre for increased scholarly activity. The appointment of the first Mackintosh Curator in 1981 instigated a project to correlate and document Mackintosh items held in the School's Collection which up until then had not been fully catalogued. Since 1981, these files have been updated chiefly through exhibitions, publications and academic theses. A notably large collection of non-Mackintosh material — paintings, prints, photographs, plaster casts, stained glass, metalwork, textiles etc., by various national and international artists — is also held by the School. Many of these items date from the initial construction of the School in 1897 and, likewise, information concerning this collection is being modified and updated.

With the appointment of a full-time Curator, every effort was made to improve the display of the Collection. The storage area above the Library was cleared and transformed into a permanent exhibition space for the housing of a major part of the Collection. While this room remains the only newly adapted display area within the School, the Mackintosh Room (formerly the Board Room), the new Board Room, the Director's Room, the Academic Registrar's Room, the Library and the Museum continue to house other items from the Collection.

The Collection itself has been compiled from three major sources: items designed specifically by Mackintosh for the School of Art — primarily furniture and internal fittings; Mackintosh artefacts kindly bequeathed, donated or gifted to the School; and additional Mackintosh items on loan to the School from private individuals and public institutions. Without doubt, the strength of the School's Collection lies in the importance and quality of many of its items and while it possesses an impressive assortment of watercolours and architectural designs, furniture comprises the bulk of the Collection.

Of all the rooms within the School, the Library remains one of the most complete and unaltered interiors. The walls of the room, on both levels, are fitted with glass-fronted bookcases. A cluster of centrally located brass and zinc lampshades (with coloured glass insets) are suspended from the wooden ceiling. These lampshades play light directly on to a striking and equally commanding periodical desk (Billcliffe: 1910.5).[1] Initially a flat reading desk, a central vertical rack was added shortly afterwards. In construction, the periodical desk with its arrangement of stretchers and particularly the latticework contained within each section, is typical of the period and as a design is repeated in the pendants which hang from the Library balcony and in the legs of the Library's square tables (B: 1910.8).

The area now occupied by the new Board Room (in a former studio to the left of the entrance hall) remains the only other interior complete with its original furniture and fitments. A large oval table of simple pine construction, stained dark brown (B: 1906.1), is still being used as are a set of twelve armchairs whose backs are carved with three horizontal crescent moon shapes (B: 1906.2).

While the original Board Room is the home for a varied and extensive collection of Mackintosh items presented to the School, the Director's Room contains both pieces designed specifically for that room and items acquired more recently by the School. The large, round central table (B: 1904.26) and its accompanying armchairs with their pierced motif of nine squares (B: 1904.28) together with the two severe high-backed armchairs (B: 1904.27) were among a number of pieces of furniture originally intended for the Director's Room. The acquisition and purchase of these particular items for the School is documented through the job-books of Honeyman & Keppie. Additional

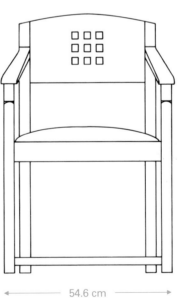

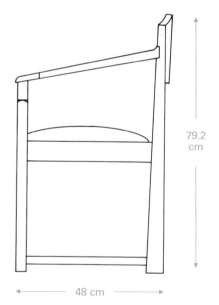

141

PERIODICAL DESK in the Library ▪
This clearly shows the wooden toggles which
hold the upright section to the original flat
table

142

ARMCHAIR with low back for the Director's
Room, 1904
Oak, 81.5 × 58.5 × 52 cm
The nine squares motif had been used in
bedroom furniture for The Hill House in 1903

Measured drawing by Jeremy Ashley

54.6 cm

48 cm

79.2
cm

correspondence contained in the minutes of the meetings of the School's Governors give an insight into disagreements that occurred with Mackintosh over the commissioning of certain items of furniture. In February 1904 the Governors called for drawings and estimates for 'some simple furniture' for the Director's Room. In March, although the style was 'generally approved with some modification', two Governors and Francis Newbery were detailed to discuss the matter with Mackintosh. In April new sketches and estimates were requested. These pieces of furniture (made by Alex Martin, a local joiner) were recorded by Mackintosh in the firm's job-books in August: 12 chairs at £12 12s; 1 circular table at £7 7s 6d; and 2 armchairs at £7 10s. When in June 1906 Mackintosh submitted a note of his fees for 1905 he showed a charge of £12 12s (about £500) for designing these items with a desk and carpet not carried out. This charge was considered too high and it was marked down by the Governors to £5 5s. Mackintosh protested about this and other reductions but to no avail. He wrote to say that he regretted he was not paid the full sum but that he was 'glad to have the opportunity of contributing the balance to the funds of the School'.

The growth and architectural development of the building during its construction is also documented. It has subsequently been enhanced by the presentation to the School from Keppie Henderson, Architects (formerly Honeyman, Keppie & Mackintosh) of a series of plans, elevations and sections of the School dating from between 1897 and 1910.

Although the items of School furniture are important in themselves, particularly when seen, still in use, in the building for which they were designed, the range and variety of artefacts now housed within the School but intended for other architectural commissions is perhaps of more significance. Thanks to the generosity of both individuals and institutions, the School now possesses examples of Mackintosh's work from various architectural projects: from his early involvement with the Glasgow firm of Guthrie & Wells in 1895 to his final designs for 78 Derngate, Northampton, and the Dug-Out in Sauchiehall Street after the First World War. A number of works including watercolours and architectural drawings have also been donated to the Collection.

As private benefactors to the School, the generosity of the artist Miss Katherine Cameron (Mrs Arthur Kay) and the extended generosity of the Davidson family (descendants of William Davidson, Mackintosh's client for Windyhill) over the last two to three decades has been particularly notable. The Cameron Bequest of 1949 presented the School with a number of Mackintosh's watercolours from the 1890s. Of the dozen or so items included in the bequest, *The Tree of Personal Effort* (1895) and *The Tree of Influence* (1895) are the most significant. These, together with *The Harvest Moon* (1892), donated to the School by Mr A. Graham Henderson (of Honeyman, Keppie & Mackintosh), epitomise Mackintosh's involvement with late nineteenth-century Symbolism and continental art nouveau.

In direct contrast to the Cameron Bequest, the generosity of the Davidson family has provided the School with an important and well-balanced collection of chiefly three-dimensional items from the houses Windyhill and Gladsmuir, both in Kilmacolm, a wealthy residential village 15 miles to the west of Glasgow. Initially, a number of large pieces of furniture were presented to the School as a result of the sale of Windyhill. Of these, the most important and visually attractive item was the sturdy bookcase (with leaded-glass door panels), designed for the drawing room at Windyhill (B: 1901.38). Since its arrival at the School, this particular bookcase has remained on permanent display in the Mackintosh Room. Its outline suggests the shape of a kimono, the collar of which has become the roof of the central niche.

Additional bequests and donations have been made by two of William Davidson's sons, Cameron and Hamish, and two of his granddaughters, Winifred and Margaret. Through the combined generosity of the Davidson family, the School now possesses two important and virtually complete suites of bedroom furniture. The first of these, comprising a bed, chest of drawers, wash-stand and dressing table with mirror date from 1895. Two of these pieces, the bed

143
THE TREE OF PERSONAL EFFORT, THE SUN OF INDIFFERENCE, 1895. Watercolour, 21.1 × 17.4 cm
This, with *The Tree of Influence*,' appeared in the spring issue of *The Magazine*, 1896

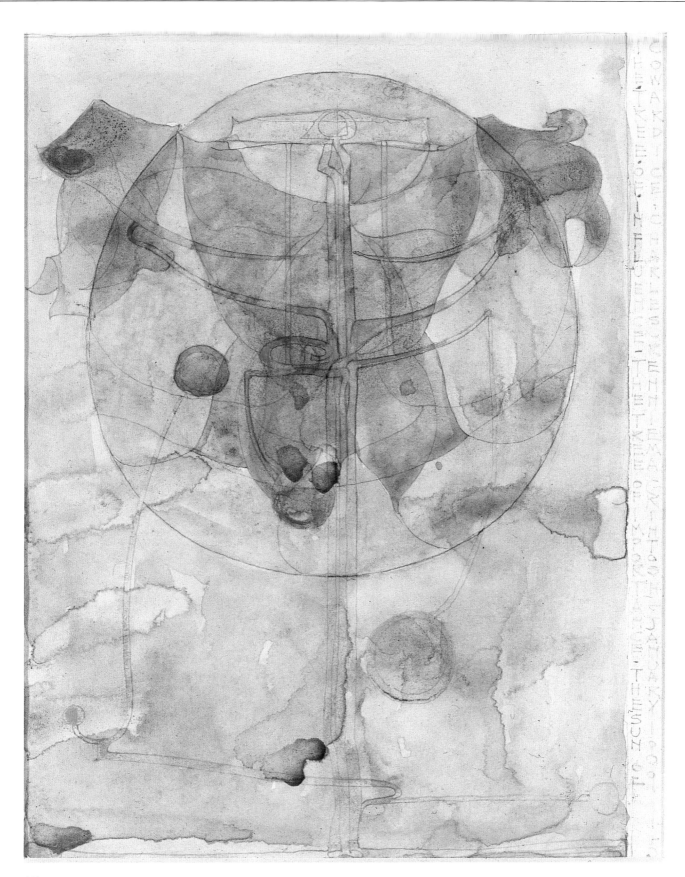

144
THE TREE OF INFLUENCE, THE TREE OF IMPORTANCE, THE SUN OF COWARDICE, 1895
Watercolour, 31.8 × 23.2 cm

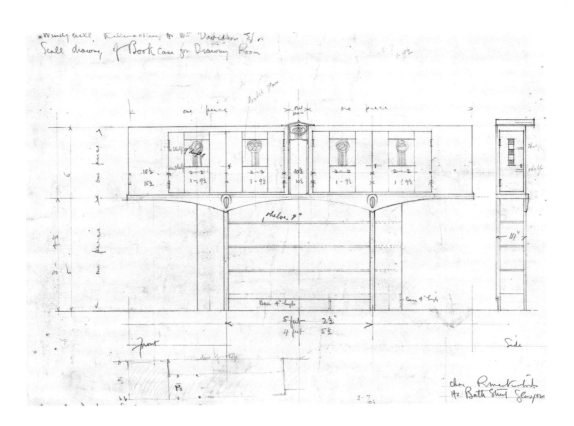

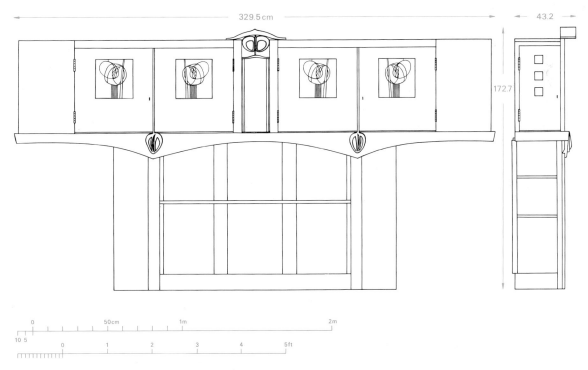

329.5 cm

43.2

172.7

| 0 | 50cm | 1m | 2m |

10 5

0 1 2 3 4 5ft

145
DESIGN FOR A BOOKCASE for Windyhill, 1901
Pencil, 26.4 × 42 cm
Presented to the School by Thomas Howarth in 1983

146
THE DRAWING-ROOM AT WINDYHILL
Photograph from *Decorative Kunst* March, 1902, p. 200
The bookcase *in situ*
Glasgow School of Art Library

147
BOOKCASE FOR WINDYHILL, 1901
Oak, with leaded glass panels, 172.5 × 329.5 × 43.2 cm

Measured drawing by Ian Macdonald

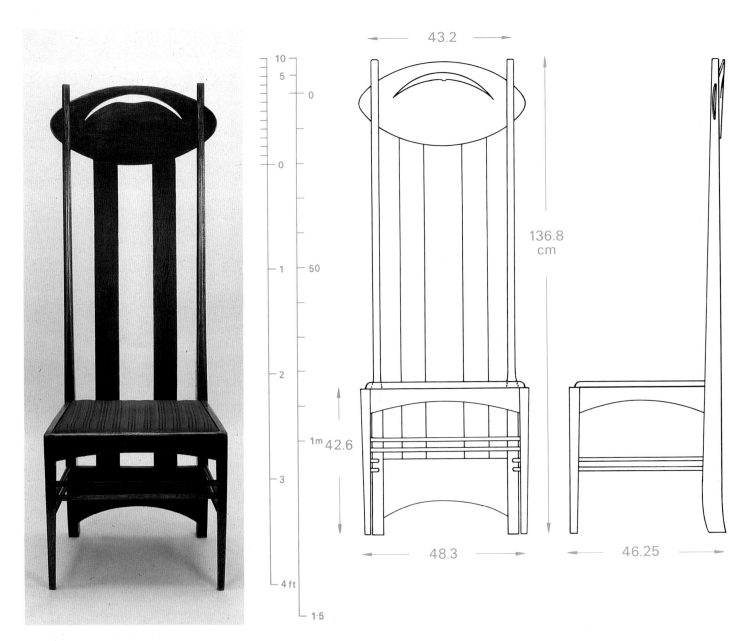

148
HIGH-BACKED CHAIR with pierced oval
backrail, 1897
Oak, 136.8 × 50.5 × 46.2 cm
Designed for the Luncheon Room in the
Argyle Street Tea Rooms

Measured drawing by Ian Macdonald

149
T & R Annan
THE DINING-ROOM, 120 Mains Street
Photograph, negative no 15391
The Chair at the Mackintoshes' dining-table
T & R Annan & Sons Ltd, Glasgow

(B: 1896.2) and the chest of drawers (B: 1896.5) would appear to have been designed by Mackintosh for use in his own flat at 27 Regent Park Square, Glasgow, with the dressing table (B: 1895.2) and the wash-stand (B: 1895.3) being acquired by Guthrie & Wells. These four pieces of furniture were then subsequently purchased by William Davidson for use in Gladsmuir.

The second of these bedroom suites was designed in 1901 for the principal bedroom at Windyhill. Unlike the earlier, more traditional, design of the Gladsmuir suite, the Windyhill furniture, enamelled in white, highlights the radical departure in Mackintosh's approach to interior decoration at the beginning of the twentieth century. As with the Gladsmuir suite, the Windyhill furniture was acquired by the School over a large number of years. The white bed (B: 1901.51) was one of the earliest pieces of Davidson furniture to be presented to the School. Since then, an accompanying wash-stand (B: 1901.44) and a highly individual cheval mirror (B: 1901.49) have also found their way to the School thanks to the Davidson family. A small white bedside table (B: 1901.47), on loan to the School from the Hunterian Art Gallery at the University of Glasgow, completes this suite of furniture.

Dark-stained schoolroom tables (B: 1897.3) and benches (B: 1897.4) from the nursery at Gladsmuir are among a number of additional items presented to the School from the Davidson family, as are the light fittings which now adorn the School's Mackintosh Room. Here, the central light fitting (constructed of sheet steel and coloured glass) was initially designed for the staircase at Windyhill, while the four square-framed lights (in both clear and lilac glass) were originally positioned in the drawing room at Windyhill. All five lights were presented to the School in 1963 as part of the Cameron Davidson Bequest.

Together with this collection of privately commissioned domestic furniture, the School has also accumulated a considerable quantity of Mackintosh's commercially designed furniture, fittings and accessories from three of Miss Cranston's Glasgow Tea Rooms. The School's earliest

acquisition of Tea Room furniture appears to date from 1954-5 through the private collection of a Mrs Napier, which included a set of high-backed chairs with pierced oval back-rails that had been used in the Luncheon Room at the Argyle Street Tea Rooms (B: 1897.23). Stylistically, these chairs were the most advanced pieces of furniture designed for the Argyle Street premises and, as such, were so successful that additional copies were used by Mackintosh in his own flat at 120 Mains Street.

Since this initial acquisition, the majority of Tea Room furniture now housed in the Collection has been acquired from two major sources: Glasgow Corporation (now Glasgow District Council) and the Grosvenor Restaurant, which had acquired the furniture from the Willow and Dug-Out Tea Rooms.

Although several pieces of Argyle Street furniture including an early table for use in the playing of dominoes (B: 1897.22) were presented to the School by Glasgow Corporation, the largest number of items from this particular source related to the Ingram Street Tea Rooms; this included a series of dark-stained chairs that were used in the White Dining Room at Ingram Street (B: 1900.54-6). Here, the format and design of one of the original chairs was modified and developed by Mackintosh into a very tall and elegant high-backed chair that was perhaps more decorative than practical (B: 1900.55).

A substantial range of additional chairs from the Ingram Street premises (including designs from both the Oak and Oval Rooms) were also presented to the School by Glasgow Corporation and in view of their more practical, sturdy nature, a number of them are now used in the Mackintosh Library (B: 1907.4, 1907.6 & 1909.14). The barrel-shaped chairs from Ingram Street (B: 1907.5) are particularly sturdy. In direct contrast, the chairs intended for the blue Chinese Room at Ingram Street (B: 1911.4) are notably elegant and refined. Despite their somewhat delicate appearance, however, these chairs are surprisingly robust and would appear to have been used in conjunction with a series of ebonised domino tables (B: 1911.5). These domino tables

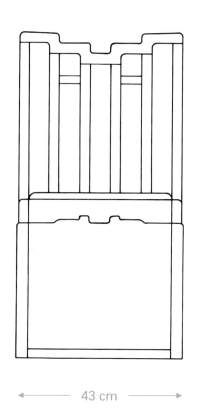

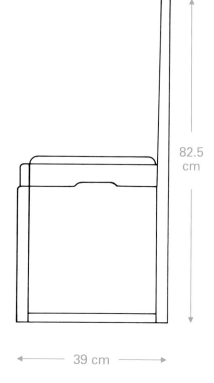

82.5 cm

← 43 cm →

← 39 cm →

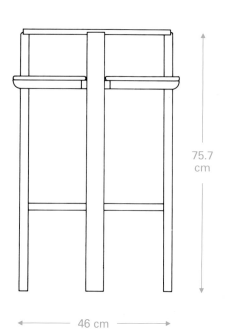

75.7 cm

← 46 cm →

150
CHAIR FOR THE CHINESE ROOM, Ingram
Street Tea Rooms, 1911
Pine, 82.4 × 43.8 × 40.7 cm
Used in a setting where much of the
woodwork was painted bright red or blue

Measured drawing by Jeremy Ashley

151
DOMINO TABLE for the Ingram Street Tea
Rooms, 1911
Oak, 77.5 × 50 × 50 cm
Probably used in conjunction with the chairs
for the Chinese Room

Measured drawing by Jeremy Ashley

are of an equally delicate appearance and are a stylistic modification of the earlier domino tables designed for the Argyle Street Tea Rooms.

In addition to this collection of Argyle and Ingram Street furniture, the School also houses an impressive assortment of furniture from the Willow and Dug-Out Tea Rooms. Begun in 1903, the Willow Tea Room was Mackintosh's most important and successful commission from Miss Cranston. A number of items presented to the School from the Grosvenor Restaurant give further emphasis to the importance of this project. The most distinctive and spectacular piece was undoubtedly the semicircular lattice chair (B: 1904.24). Decorated with a highly stylised willow tree motif, this particular chair was designed as a division between the Tea Room's Front and Back Salons. This superb chair had a mundane function; here the manageress dealt with customers' orders. An additional selection of Tea Room furniture, ladderback chairs (B: 1903.8), waitress stools (B: 1903.13) and a table (B: 1903.37) together with a severely geometric longcase clock (B: 1903.31), were also acquired from the Grosvenor Restaurant. Despite its relative scarcity, the School also received a selection of silver-painted furniture from the Willow's Room de Luxe (B: 1903.26 & 1904.23); Mackintosh's most innovative and sophisticated tea room interior.

Mackintosh's final commission for Miss Cranston was for a Tea Room in Glasgow in 1917. Known as the Dug-Out (in view of its construction during wartime in the basement of the building adjoining the existing Willow Tea Rooms), the majority of its furniture was also donated to the School by the Grosvenor Restaurant. Tea Room tables (B: 1917.32 & 1917.33) and ladderback chairs (B: 1917.35 & 1917.36) form the bulk of this collection but the largest and most significant item from the Dug-Out remains the bright yellow settle (B: 1917.30). The style and colouring of this settle (with its purple upholstery) is typical of Mackintosh's later interior designs which have strong links with art deco.

Although the majority of the School's Mackintosh Collection has been secured through various large-scale acquisitions, a number of important pieces have been presented or bequeathed to the School as part of smaller often single donations. These have included Mackintosh's own presentation to the School in 1908 of a portfolio of his printed designs from the *Haus eines Kunstfreundes* (House for an Art Lover) competition. The large smoker's cabinet (B: 1903.1), presented to the School by Mrs Napier, is a replica of the cabinet exhibited by Mackintosh at the Vienna Secession in 1900 (B: 1899.1). The Director's writing desk is somewhat unusual. It was designed by Mackintosh (B: 1904.29) but never built during his lifetime. In 1986, using Mackintosh's original design, Donald and Eleanor Taffner of New York (who are supporting financially the post of the Mackintosh Curator) had the desk constructed and then presented it to the School. A small number of items by Margaret Macdonald have also been presented to the School and these include the gesso panel *Heart of the Rose* and the two embroidered panels exhibited in Turin during 1902.

The cost of purchasing Mackintosh furniture presents problems for today's collector. With only a limited number of pieces available, every item that appears on the market becomes highly sought after. In 1904, Mackintosh designed a writing desk for the Blue Bedroom at Miss Cranston's Hous'hill (B: 1904.80). Constructed on similar lines to the piece intended for the Director's Room at the School of Art, the Hous'hill desk was auctioned at Sotheby's in London on 21 October 1988 for £82,500 (including buyer's premium).

This dramatic rise in value of Mackintosh's work can also be seen in the sale of his watercolours and drawings. During his own lifetime, these items were valued at little more than a few pounds but in view of their scarcity today, a single watercolour can easily command a price over and above that achieved by the sale of a piece of furniture.

In an attempt to complement its own permanent Mackintosh Collection, the School continues to maintain long-standing exchange agreements with a variety of individual institutions. This allows for works of art to be loaned to and from the School of Art for varying lengths of time, over and above the normal duration of any temporary exhibition.

153
T & R Annan
Photograph
FRONT SALON, The Willow Tea Rooms,
1904   □ ■
The high curved back of the chair, seen in
the background to the right, acts as a
division between the front and back Salons

Hunterian Art Gallery, University of Glasgow,
Mackintosh Collection

152
CURVED LATTICE-BACK CHAIR for
The Willow Tea Rooms, 1904
Oak, 118.7 × 94 × 42.2 cm
Perhaps Mackintosh's most impressive and
original furniture design

Measured drawing by Ian Macdonald

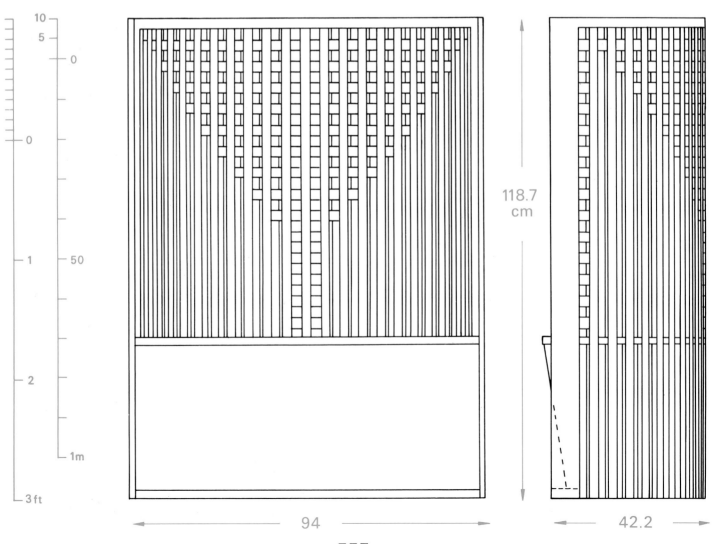

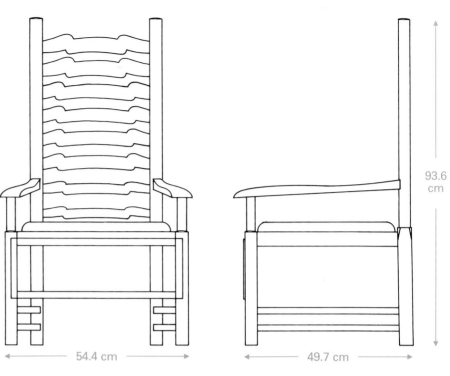

93.6 cm

54.4 cm

49.7 cm

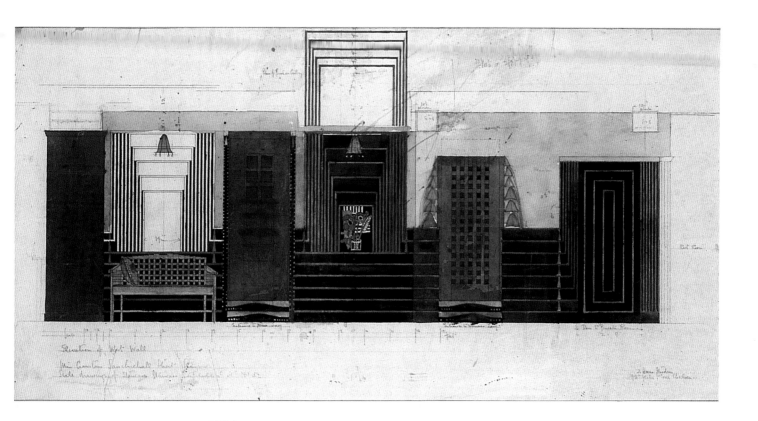

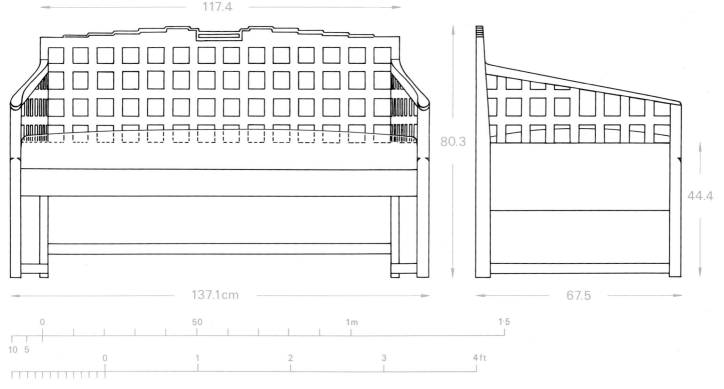

117.4

80.3

44.4

137.1cm

67.5

154

LARGE LADDERBACK ARMCHAIR for the
Dug-Out, Willow Tea Rooms, 1917
Ebonised wood, 93.7 × 58.5 × 52.2 cm
A smaller version, with rounded arms, was
also designed for the Dug-Out

Measured drawing by Jeremy Ashley

155

SETTLE FOR THE DUG-OUT, Willow Tea
Rooms, 1917
Enamelled wood, 79.5 × 137 × 70.4 cm
As the design for the Dug-Out shows
the settle was intended for the staircase
vestibule

156

DESIGN FOR THE DUG-OUT, Willow Tea
Rooms, 1917
Watercolour, 40.2 × 76.5 cm
The scheme, produced at Glebe Place,
Chelsea, uses bright primary colours. The
settle, as shown here, has longer legs than it
has now

Measured drawing by Ian Macdonald

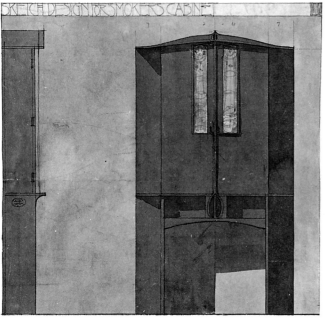

157
DESIGN FOR A SMOKER'S CABINET, 1899
Pencil, 10.2 × 15.1 cm
Perhaps the first noted thoughts on the design; to the right is a sketch for the light over the School steps
Hunterian Art Gallery, University of Glasgow,
Mackintosh Collection

158
SKETCH DESIGN FOR A SMOKER'S CABINET, 1899
Watercolour, 32.2 × 35.2 cm
This relates to the first of the two executed cabinets
Hunterian Art Gallery, University of Glasgow,
Mackintosh Collection

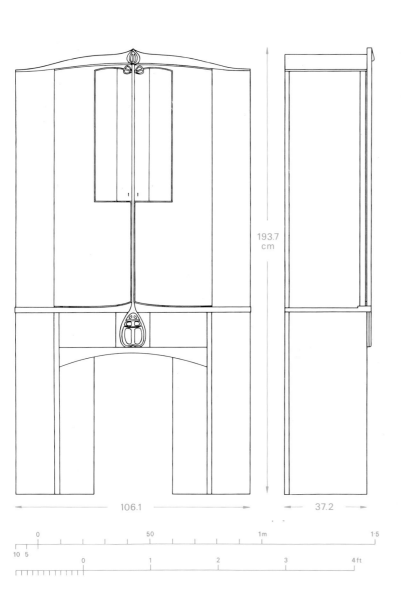

159
SMOKER'S CABINET, 1903
Oak, with beaten copper panels by Margaret
Macdonald Mackintosh, 194.8 × 106 × 38.8 cm
This is a replica, for Mackintosh's own use, of
the cabinet sold to Hugo Henneberg in Vienna in 1900

Measured drawing by Ian Macdonald

160
SELECTION OF FURNITURE displayed in
the Director's office

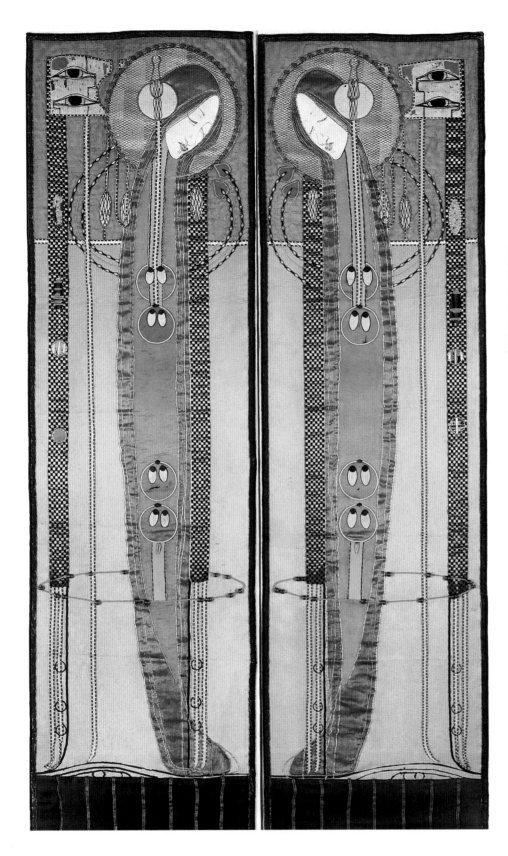

162
Margaret Macdonald Mackintosh
PAIR OF EMBROIDERED PANELS for The
Hill House, 1902
Linen with silk, metal, braid, ribbon, beads,
each 182.2 × 40.6 cm
These may be duplicates of those shown in
Vienna in 1900 and in Turin in 1902

At present, the Hunterian Art Gallery at the University of Glasgow, the Glasgow Art Gallery and Museum, the National Museums of Scotland in Edinburgh and the Central Museum in Northampton are all actively involved. It is an agreement that, it is hoped, will continue for it not only enriches the School's permanent collection but allows other institutions to benefit from the School's varied and important Mackintosh Collection.

NOTES

1   This reference (B: 1910.5), together with subsequent entries listed as (B: —), relates to the numbering system employed by Roger Billcliffe in his publication, *Charles Rennie Mackintosh: The Complete Furniture, Furniture Drawings and Interior Designs*, John Murray, 3rd edn., 1986.

COMPUTER PROJECTIONS OF THE SCHOOL

MIKE
STRANG

These orthogonal projections, where each dimension is in correct proportion to the others, were created on a Compaq 286 computer using AutoCAD. The completed building is based on data taken from a set of nine undated drawings (1910) marked in Mackintosh's own hand 'Honeyman Keppie & Mackintosh/ Architects/ 4 Blythswood Square Glasgow.' The first phase of the building was reconstructed from this projection and from further information gleaned from drawings and plans.

1 PHASE 1

a View from the North-East

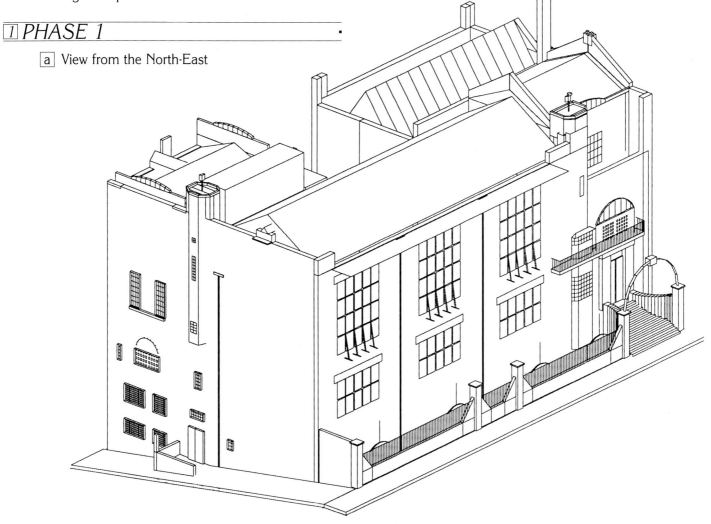

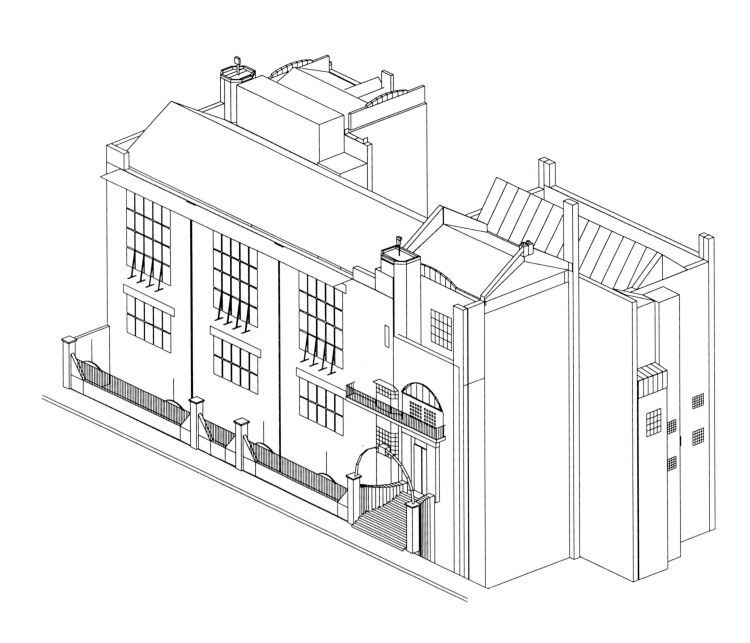

b View from the North-West

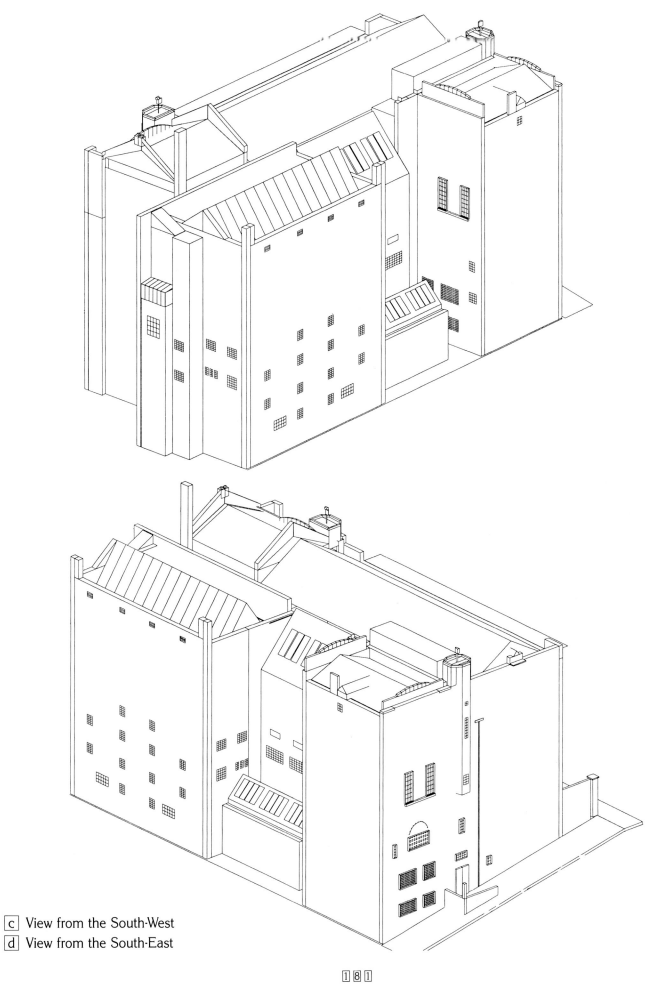

c View from the South-West
d View from the South-East

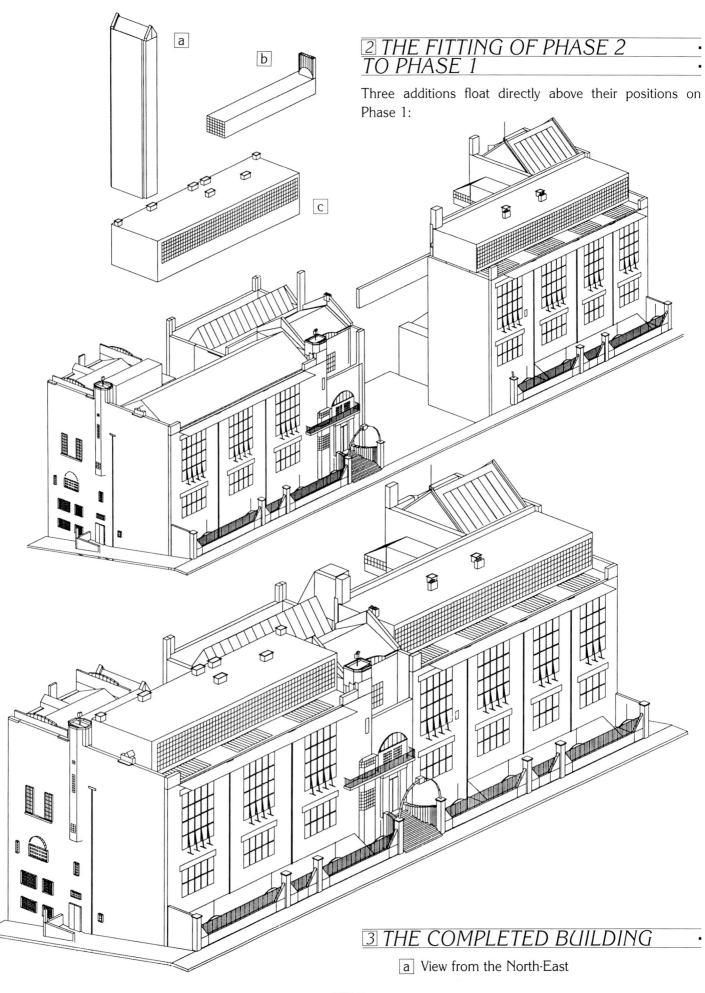

Three additions float directly above their positions on Phase 1:

a

b

c

3 THE COMPLETED BUILDING

a View from the North-East

a East Staircase, which runs across the Board Room windows.

b The Pavilion, which connects the two phases of the building behind the top of the Director's studio.

c Attic Studios. The sloping roof on Phase 1 was taken off and the studios added, breaking into part of the roof space in the studios beneath. Top lights were added to these studios to match those in Phase 2.

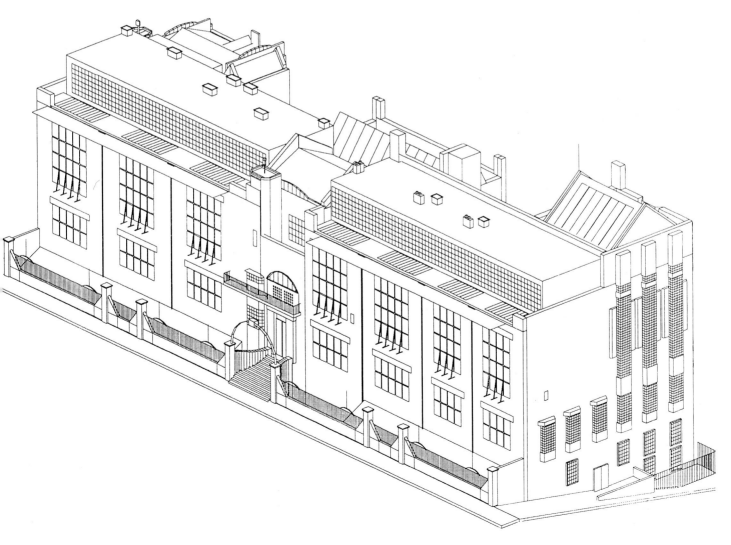

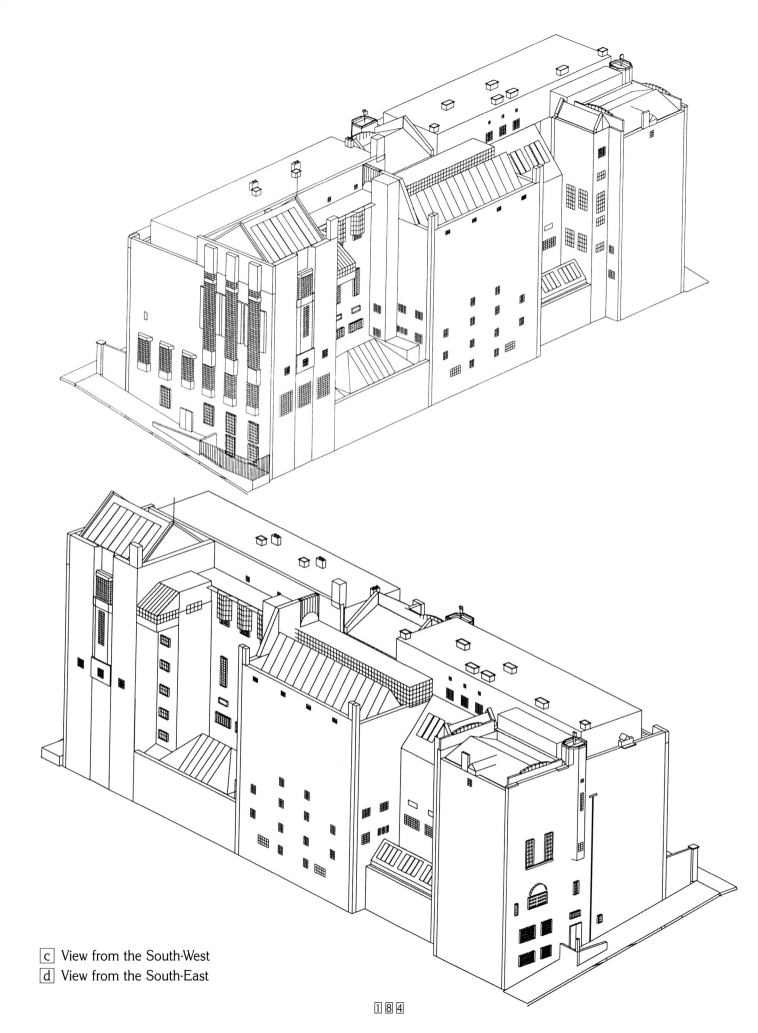

c View from the South-West

d View from the South-East

BIBLIOGRAPHY
WITH ANNOTATIONS

THIS bibliography is a chronological listing of published and unpublished material, relating to Mackintosh's Glasgow School of Art building and does not deal with his other work.[1] The early references, especially, contain a large quantity of unpublished material, and locations for these are given. The bibliography aims to be as comprehensive as possible, as far as books and journal articles are concerned, but it also contains a selection of reports from Glasgow newspapers, where these are the only source of information on the building's planning and construction. A chronological treatment has been chosen because it highlights the interest which was taken in the building during and immediately after its erection and serves to bring out the growing amount of critical acclaim which it has attracted since the architect's death. It might seem strange that although much of Mackintosh's architectural and design work was well covered in contemporary periodicals, both in Britain and Europe, during his lifetime, the Art School itself hardly appeared at all in their pages. No photographs of the exterior seem to have been published until 1933,[2] and no plans, outside the School's own prospectuses, until 1950. *The Studio* published a review of the building (as the work of Honeyman & Keppie), with four photographs of the interior, in 1900, but these, and the article which they illustrate, concentrate on the School as an educational institution, rather than as a work of architecture. From Mackintosh's death until the later 1930s almost all references to the School were extremely short and uninformative. The lack of publicity must certainly have done much to prevent this revolutionary building from exerting the influence, which it otherwise might have had, over Modernist architects, in the first few decades of the twentieth century.

Nikolaus Pevsner must take the credit for re-awakening an interest in Mackintosh and bringing the Art School before a wider public, in his *Pioneers of the Modern Movement*, which appeared in 1936, and in the first short monograph on the architect, published in Italian, in 1950. These were followed, in 1952, by Thomas Howarth's indispensable standard work, published in London and New York, which besides containing a full discussion of the School and the history of its building, was also well illustrated with plans and photographs. This, in its turn, was followed, in 1968, by Robert Macleod's excellent, well-illustrated study. Also, during the 1960s, the Art School published three short companion volumes on the building and its contents, and Mackintosh's centenary year, coming in 1968, witnessed an important exhibition, staged in Edinburgh, London, Darmstadt and Vienna, as well as a crop of articles on different aspects of his life and work.

The 1970s saw the first measured study of a part of the School, when the Italian periodical *Casabella* featured a set of drawings of the Library. This has since been followed by a series of similar surveys of other parts of the building, undertaken by the Mackintosh School of Architecture, as student dissertations. The most significant student work, however, was the doctoral thesis, completed in 1982, by Hiroaki Kimura, many of whose findings were later published in the Japanese periodical, *Process Architecture*, in 1984. Apart from compiling a catalogue of all Mackintosh's known architectural drawings, the author also included an analysis of the evolution of the design of the Art School, based on a comparison of the drawings of the building produced during the course of its construction. Interest in the architect and his masterwork has continued to grow into the present decade, and perhaps the best indication of their current standing among architects was the readers' poll, conducted by the British architectural weekly, *Building Design*, in March 1984. This voted Mackintosh as the best British architect of the last 150 years, and the Glasgow School of Art as the best building.

NOTES

1 A good general bibliography was published in London by the Architectural Association in 1981: *Charles Rennie Mackintosh (1868-1928): a selective bibliography* compiled by Elizabeth Dixon (A. A. Library Bibliography [new series No. 55]).

2 There is a reference to a photograph of the Library wing appearing in an unspecified source in 1909, given on pp. 253-4 of Howarth's book.

163
T & R Annan
WEST FAÇADE OF THE SCHOOL, n d
Photograph
Probably the earliest published exterior view
of the School. See the Bibliography, under
the entry for 1933
Glasgow School of Art Library

1879   GLASGOW SCHOOL OF ART

Annual Reports 1879-1906 and 1906-17.

Glasgow: Glasgow School of Art, 2 vols.
Background information on the need for a new Art School
building and progress of the building itself.
Location: Glasgow School of Art Library.

1883   GLASGOW SCHOOL OF ART

Building fund cash book, 1883-1905.

Unpublished manuscript.
Location: Glasgow School of Art Library.

1892   THE BRITISH ARCHITECT

The Glasgow art galleries competition.

The British Architect, vol. 37, June 1892, pp. 426, 432-3.
Mackintosh submitted an entry for this competition under the
name of his employers, Honeyman & Keppie. The art school
on the west side of the plan can be compared with his later
Glasgow School of Art.

1893   GLASGOW SCHOOL OF ART

Prospectuses, 1893-4 − 1913-14.

Glasgow: Glasgow School of Art.
These give information on the progress of the building and on
the teaching methods which it was designed to cater for. The
1907-8 prospectus contains plans based on those of 1897, with
unbuilt extension shaded: the prospectus for 1909-10 contains
plans of the completed building.
Location: Glasgow School of Art Library.

1894   HONEYMAN & KEPPIE

Job books, c.1894-1904, c.1904-10.

Unpublished manuscript, 2 vols.
The architects' day-to-day records of building work done on
the Art School, and the charges made for it. Entries for the
School are on pp. 121-32 of vol. 1 and pp. 46, 155-64 and 176-
7 of vol. 2.
Location: Keppie Henderson, Architects, Glasgow.

1895   DEPARTMENT OF SCIENCE & ART

Directory, Science and Art Schools and classes, 1895.

Department of Science and Art, 1895.
On pp. 116-17 are printed 'Regulations under which building
grants are made to Schools of Science and Art'. This
document was used by Newbery as a basis for the competition
brief.

GLASGOW HERALD

The Glasgow School of Art: proposed new building.

Glasgow Herald, 7 March 1895.
Report on a memorial sent by the School's governors to the
Town Council regarding their proposal to build a new Art
School on the Renfrew Street site.

GLASGOW SCHOOL OF ART: Board of Governors

Minute books, nos 4-7, March 1895-June 1911.

Unpublished manuscript.
Important source for background to competition and progress
of building.
Location: Glasgow School of Art Library.

1896   GLASGOW SCHOOL OF ART

Conditions of the competition of architects for the proposed
new School of Art.

Glasgow: Glasgow School of Art, June 1896, 6 pp.
[privately printed].
The competition brief, prepared by Newbery.
Location: Glasgow School of Art Library.

GLASGOW SCHOOL OF ART: Board of Governors:
Building Committee

Minute Book, 1896-9.

Unpublished manuscript.
Important source for the progress of the first stage of the
building.
Location: Glasgow School of Art Library.

1897   GLASGOW HERALD

Public notices: The Glasgow School of Art: designs for the
proposed new School of Art building.

Glasgow Herald, 1 February 1897.
Advertisement for the exhibition of the competition drawings
in the Corporation Galleries, 1-16 February 1897.

SCOTT, Robert

Estimates for the building works for the construction of
the Glasgow School of Art/prepared by Robert Scott,
115 Wellington Street, Glasgow.

Unpublished manuscript, 1897.
10 estimates: no 1, excavator mason and brickworks; no 2, cast
iron work; no 3, steel work; no 4, carpenter and joiner works;
no 5, glazier work; no 6, slater work; no 7, plumber work;
no 8, gasfitter work; [no 9, missing]; no 10, marble and works;

painter work [unnumbered], and general specification and
description of heating and ventilating.
Location: Glasgow School of Art Library.

THE BUILDER

The Glasgow School of Art.

The Builder, vol. 72, 6 March 1897, pp. 228-9.
Description of layout of Mackintosh's winning scheme.

DAILY RECORD

Glasgow School of Art: new buildings to be erected.

Daily Record, 1 October 1897.
Records acceptance of tenders for new building.

1898 ## THE BAILIE

Men you know [Mr Francis H. Newbery: Headmaster,
Glasgow School of Art].

The Bailie, vol. 52, no 1336, 25 May 1898, pp. 1-2 and 5.
Short biographical article on Newbery, with portrait, published
on the occasion of the laying of the memorial stone of the
new Art School building.

EVENING TIMES

[Sketch of laying of Memorial Stone ceremony.]

Evening Times, 26 May 1898.

GLASGOW HERALD

Glasgow School of Art.

Glasgow Herald, 26 May 1898.
Records the ceremony of the laying of the memorial stone of
the new building, with some account of the contemplated
accommodation.

BUILDING NEWS

The Glasgow School of Art.

Building News, vol. 75, 26 August 1898, p. 306.
A short article on the institution, its staff, its achievements
and the laying of the memorial stone of its new building.

DAILY RECORD

The Glasgow School of Art.

Daily Record, 11 October 1898.
Notes that the School has taken possession of the new
building.

1899 ## EVENING TIMES

Opening of the School of Art.

Evening Times, 21 September 1899.
A report of the opening ceremony, with an accompanying
drawing of the exterior from the north-east.

1900 ## 'SCOTIA'

Scottish society notes: Glasgow School of Art.

Madame, 6 January 1900, p. 15.
An account of the opening of the School as a social event,
with fashion comments.

BUILDING INDUSTRIES AND SCOTTISH ARCHITECT

[The Glasgow School of Art.]

Building Industries and Scottish Architect, 16 January 1900,
pp. 146-7, 153.
A not altogether favourable review of the first stage,
accompanied by a rather stiff drawing of the building from the
north-east, which fails to include the wrought-iron finials on
the roof.

THE STUDIO

[Glasgow School of Art.]

The Studio, vol. 19, 15 February 1900, pp. 48-56.
Description of accommodation with 4 photographs of the
interior, by Annan: museum; east corridor on first floor;
2 studios. The only photographs of interiors of the building
to be published in Mackintosh's lifetime. These are not
distinctive from an architectural point of view.

1902 ## MUTHESIUS, Hermann

Die Glasgower Kunstbewung: Charles R. Mackintosh und
Margaret Macdonald Mackintosh.

Dekorative Kunst, vol. 6, March 1902, pp. 193-217.
Contains an illustration of the relief panel over the main
doorway, modelled by Mackintosh for copying by the stone-
carvers.

1903 ## GLASGOW HERALD

The presentation panel to Mr James Fleming.

Glasgow Herald, 17 January 1903.
Records the presentation of the panel, made by George
Frampton with a surround by Mackintosh, on the main
stairway of the building.

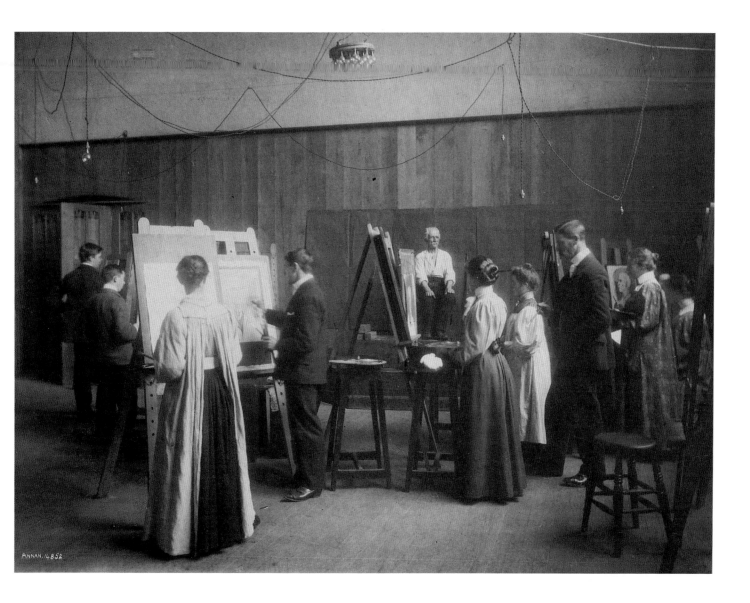

EVENING TIMES

Prominent profiles: Art School [Francis Henry Newbery].

Evening Times, 25 November 1903.
Short biographical sketch and portrait.

1905   GLASGOW SCHOOL OF ART

Letterbook, 1905-10.

Unpublished manuscript.
Contains letters, 1907-10, between Mackintosh and the
Building Committee on the second stage of the building.
Location: Glasgow School of Art Library.

1906   GLASGOW HERALD

The Glasgow School of Art: the completion of building,
handsome gift.

Glasgow Herald, 5 November 1906.
Notes a gift towards the building fund, but is mainly about the
lack of accommodation for many departments in the first
stage of the building.

GLASGOW SCHOOL OF ART: Board of Governors:
Building Committee

Extensions and alterations: minute book no 1, 1906-7, and
minute book no 2, 1908-11, 2 vols.

Unpublished manuscript.
Important source for the progress of the second stage of the
building and for Mackintosh's relations with the Building
Committee.
Location: Glasgow School of Art Library.

1907   SCOTT, Robert

Glasgow School of Art: extensions and alterations/prepared
by Robert Scott, 115 Wellington Street, Glasgow.

Unpublished manuscript, 1907-8.
2 estimates: no 1, excavator mason and brickworks; no 8,
heating and ventilating apparatus.
Location: Glasgow School of Art Library.

GLASGOW HERALD

Glasgow School of Art extension scheme.

Glasgow Herald, 26 January 1907.
A note on recent subscriptions received towards the sum
required to start the second stage.

165
J. M. Hamilton
SCHOOL OF ART
'Mr Newbery is a gentleman of remarkable
energy, and possesses unusual powers as an
organiser.' 'Prominent Profiles', *Evening
Times*, 25 Nov. 1903
Glasgow School of Art Library

166
J. M. Hamilton
ART AND POLITICS
The palette and the vase refer to Sir James
Fleming as Managing Director of the
Britannia Pottery, St Rollox, and Chairman of
the Board of the School. 'Prominent Profiles',
Evening Times, 14 Aug. 1907
Glasgow School of Art Library

GLASGOW HERALD
Glasgow School of Art: sketch of proposed extension.

Glasgow Herald, 26 January 1907.
Shows School from north-west, more or less as it would
appear when completed, but without the attic storey.

EVENING TIMES
Prominent profiles: art and politics [Sir James Fleming].

Evening Times, 14 August 1907.
Short biographical sketch and portrait of the Chairman of the
Board of Governors.

GLASGOW SCHOOL OF ART
Building fund contracts ledger, 1907-9.

Unpublished manuscript.
Location: Glasgow School of Art Library.

1909   GLASGOW NEWS

School of Art Club: students' annual exhibition.

Glasgow News, 20 February 1909.
Mentions that the exhibition was held in the basement of the 'still uncompleted addition'.

GLASGOW NEWS

EVENING TIMES

Prominent profiles: architecture [Charles Rennie Mackintosh].

Evening Times, 11 December 1909.
Drawing of Mackintosh with a short biography as the architect of the new School of Art building.

GLASGOW HERALD

Glasgow School of Art: opening of new building.

Glasgow Herald, 15 December 1909.
Records celebrations which were held to mark the opening of the building.

BUILDING INDUSTRIES AND SCOTTISH ARCHITECT

Glasgow School of Art.

Building Industries and Scottish Architect, 16 December 1909, pp. 130-1.
Another article on the festivities accompanying the opening of the building, with same drawing of the first stage, from the north-east, which was used in this periodical's article of January 1900 (q.v.).

GLASGOW NEWS

School of Art: opening celebrations: Birth and growth of art.

Glasgow News, 18 December 1909.
Describes the masque performed by the staff and students of the School as part of the opening celebrations.

1914   THE SCOTS PICTORIAL

'The Governors of the Glasgow School of Art' [sic] from the painting by Fra H. Newbery.

The Scots Pictorial, 30 May 1914, p. 230.
An illustration of Newbery's group portrait of the Building Committee.

1928   THE TIMES

Obituary: C. R. Mackintosh: pioneer of modernist architecture.

The Times, 14 December 1928, p. 16.
Regards the Glasgow School of Art as Mackintosh's most important building.

GLASGOW HERALD

Notable Glasgow architect: late Charles Rennie Mackintosh.

An appreciation by J. Jeffrey Waddell.

Glasgow Herald, 15 December 1928.
An overview of the architect's career. Contains some errors. Mentions the School of Art and notes his high standing in Europe.

1929   ARCHITECTURAL REVIEW

C. R. Mackintosh: obituary.

Architectural Review, vol. 65, January 1929, p. 54.

ROBERTSON, Howard

Obituary: the contribution of Charles Rennie Mackintosh.

Royal Institute of British Architects Journal, vol. 56, 12 January 1929, p. 211.
Sees the Art School as Mackintosh's most important building. Regards it as a precursor of modernism, in its external treatment and interior details.

TAUT, Bruno

Modern Architecture.

London: *The Studio,* 1929, 212 pp.
Briefly mentions Mackintosh, but carries 3 fine illustrations of the Art School, from photographs by Bedford Lemere, 2 interiors of Library and 1 interior of an attic storey studio. These were published 'by courtesy of Mrs Mackintosh'.

1930   CHAPMAN-HUSTON, Desmond

Charles Rennie Mackintosh.

Artwork, vol. 6, no 21, Spring 1930, pp. 21-31.
Highly appreciative biographical sketch by this friend of Mackintosh, with some mention of the Art School commission. Features a photograph of the entrance hall by Bedford Lemere.

1933   ALLAN GLEN'S MAGAZINE

Charles Rennie Mackintosh: a great architect, 1868-1928.

Allan Glen's Magazine, Midsummer 1933, pp. 18-19.
An appreciation of Mackintosh in the magazine of his old school, prompted by the Memorial Exhibition of that year.

MACKIE, Campbell

Charles Rennie Mackintosh.

The Builder, vol. 145, no 4718, 7 July 1933, p. 8.
An appreciation of Mackintosh as a forerunner of modernism.
The School is not mentioned, but there is an illustration from
Annan's photograph of the Library wing. This was probably
the first exterior photograph to be published.

MAINDS, Alan D.

Charles Rennie Mackintosh.

The Listener, vol. 10, no 236, 19 July 1933, pp. 98-100.
Written by a former student and teacher in the Art School.
Has little to say about the building beyond seeing it as a
landmark in the history of architecture and as a forerunner of
the Modern Movement. Also has photograph of Library wing.

McLELLAN GALLERIES

Charles Rennie Mackintosh, Margaret Macdonald
Mackintosh: Memorial Exhibition.

Glasgow: McLellan Galleries, 1933.

Not significant for its content on the Art School, but it helped
to excite more interest in Mackintosh's work. Some
photographs of the School, by Bedford Lemere, were included
in the exhibition.

TAYLOR, E. A.

Charles Rennie Mackintosh: a neglected genius.

The Studio, vol. 105, 1933, pp. 344-52.
By a friend of Mackintosh. Contains some passing mention of
Taylor's perception of the response of Glasgow architects to
the Art School building.

WADDELL, J. Jeffrey

Charles Rennie Mackintosh: the man and his work: an
appreciation.

*Quarterly Illustrated of the Royal Incorporation of Architects in
Scotland,* no 42, Spring 1933, pp. 11-14.
An informative piece on Mackintosh's career, but with only a
few sentences on the Art School. Illustrated with a
photograph of the Library wing, taken by Annan.

1935   CHAPMAN-HUSTON, Desmond
Charles Rennie Mackintosh.

London: Royal Institute of British Architects.
Handbook of the British Architects' Conference at Glasgow,
1935, pp. 81-9.
A reprint of Chapman-Huston's article in *Artwork* (1930), but
this time illustrated with a drawing of the School from the
north-west by Alexander McGibbon.

SHAND, P. Morton
Glasgow interlude.

Architectural Review, vol. 77, January 1935, pp. 23-6.
An attempt to establish what modernism owed to Mackintosh.
The Art School, discussed in this context, on p. 26, is regarded
as 'by far the most original architectural design of its day, but
structurally much behind contemporary engineering practice'.
Includes 2 photographs of the School: a view of the north
façade and Library interior, by Bedford Lemere.

1936   PEVSNER, Nikolaus
Pioneers of the modern movement: from William Morris to
Walter Gropius.

London: Faber & Faber, 1936, 240 pp.
There is an analysis of the Art School building on pp. 158-65
with 3 photographs: the north façade; the Library interior; the
west wing. This is the earliest appreciation of Mackintosh and
the Art School building in book form.

SCOTTISH DAILY EXPRESS
The talk of Glasgow.

Scottish Daily Express, 30 September 1936.
Mentions the lightening of the dark stained timber in the
main staircase.

1940   GROUNDWATER, John M.
The Glasgow School of Art through a century, 1840-1940.

Glasgow: Glasgow School of Art, 1940, 14 pp.
The only attempt at a history of the institution. Though full of
inaccuracies for the early years, the information on the
building of Mackintosh's school is reasonably correct. The
frontispiece is Annan's photograph of the west wing.

RICHARDS, J. M.
Modern Architecture.

Harmondsworth: Penguin Books, 1940, 176 pp.
Page 68 sees the School's interior as a British example of art
nouveau. There is one photograph of the north façade.

1947   BLISS, Douglas Percy
His eye on the stars.

Scottish Field, July 1947, pp. 24-5.
The article carries 7 illustrations of the School, mostly
interiors photographed at the time.

1949   CHAPMAN-HUSTON, Desmond
The Lamp of Memory: autobiographical digressions.

London: Skeffington, 1949.
Pages 124-9 and 141 discuss Mackintosh. On p. 126 his
difficulties with the Building Committee of the School are
mentioned.

HOWARTH, Thomas
Charles Rennie Mackintosh and the secessionist movement in
architecture.

Glasgow University PhD Thesis no 935, 1949 – 2 vols.,
315 pp.
Chapter 3 of vol. 1 is devoted to the Art School. The history
and progress of the building is chronicled, together with a
lengthy description of the main features. Very well illustrated
with plans and photographs, this study formed the basis for
Howarth's later standard work on Mackintosh.
Location: University of Glasgow Library.

1950   GODWIN, W. G. J.
Rennie Mackintosh, Victor Horta and Berlage.

Architectural Association Journal, February 1950, pp. 140-5.
Discusses the Art School building on p. 145.

HOWARTH, Thomas
Charles Rennie Mackintosh (1868-1928): architect and
designer.

Royal Institute of British Architects' Journal, vol. 58, 1950,
pp. 15-19.
Edited manuscript of a talk broadcast on the BBC Third
Programme. Looks at Mackintosh's work against the
background of his time and sees the School as innovative but
within the Scottish tradition. Includes 2 illustrations of the
building.

168
Herbert Spencer □■□
COVER of Nikolaus Pevsner, *Pioneers of Modern Design: From William Morris to Walter Gropious*, Penguin, 1960 (rev. edn.)
The School in its international context: Eiffel's Tower, Paris, 1890; Olbrich's Wedding Tower, Darmstadt, 1907; Gropius & Meyer's Factory for the Werkbund Exhibition, Cologne, 1914
Penguin Books Ltd

169
Gordon Huntly □□■
COVER of Andrew McLaren Young and A. M. Doak (eds.), *Glasgow at a Glance: An Architectural Handbook*, Collins, 1965
The School in the context of the city: Glasgow Cathedral, early 13th century onwards; Alexander Thomson's St Vincent Street Church, 1858; the arms of Scotland and of Glasgow from beaten metal panels on a building by James Salmon, Jnr, at 24 West Regent Street   *William Collins plc*

PEVSNER, Nikolaus
C. R. Mackintosh.

Milan: Il Balcone, 1950 – 152 pp. (Architetti del Movimento Moderno, no 8).
The first monograph on Mackintosh. It contains a description and analysis of the School together with 9 illustrations of it. This was the first publication (apart from the Art School prospectuses of the 1900s (q.v.)) to include a plan: this is of the 1st floor, and is contemporary with the book. Text in Italian.

TONGE, John
Charles Rennie Mackintosh: Celtic innovator.

Scottish Art Review, vol. 3, no 1, 1950, pp. 13-17.
Another short biography with some comment on the School. Includes 2 illustrations of the building.

1951   SMITH, William
Architecture, Glasgow and Mackintosh.

Proceedings of the Royal Philosophical Society of Glasgow, vol. 75, part 6, 1951, pp. 55-67.

1952   HOWARTH, Thomas
Charles Rennie Mackintosh and the Modern Movement.

London: Routledge & Kegan Paul, 1952, 329 pp. (Glasgow University publications, 94).
The standard work on Mackintosh, based on Howarth's PhD thesis of 1949 (q.v.). The School of Art is dealt with at length on pp. 69-92 and is also well illustrated, with interior and exterior photographs, plans, sections and elevations of the School as built, and at different stages of planning, all from Mackintosh's drawings.

SUMMERSON, John
[Review of Howarth's Charles Rennie Mackintosh and the Modern Movement.]

New Statesman & Nation, 27 December 1952, pp. 784-5.
Offers Summerson's own views on Mackintosh and the Glasgow School of Art; 'the architecture of the *fin de siècle* neurosis'.

1953   DEL RENZIO, Toni
Charles Rennie Mackintosh: the Glasgow School.

World Review, June 1953, pp. 23-7.

Pages 25-6 contain an admiring appreciation of the Art School, 'the most modern building in Great Britain'.

FLEMING, J. Arnold
A tribute to Charles MacIntosh [sic].

Scottish Journal, no 6, February/March/April 1953, p. 6.
Written by the son of the Chairman of Governors of the School during its building. He indicates that his father was a firm supporter of the architect.

HOWARTH, Thomas
Charles Rennie Mackintosh, 1868-1928.

Edinburgh: Saltire Society with Arts Council of Great Britain, 1953, 13 pp.
The first comprehensive exhibition of Mackintosh's work since 1933, it contained some material on the School including models of the School and of the Library.

1954   HOWARTH, Thomas
Mackintosh and Scottish architecture.

Saltire Review, no 1, April 1954, pp. 23-7.
Looks at Mackintosh and the Art School against the background of the Scottish vernacular tradition.

1959   SHAND, P. Morton
C. R. Mackintosh.

Architectural Association Journal, vol. 75, January 1959, pp. 163-7.
Reprint of article of 1935 in *Architectural Review* (q.v.).

1960   BANHAM, Reyner
Alienation of the parts.

New Statesman, 5 March 1960, pp. 331-2.
A wittily observed and lively description of the School. 'The weirdest building I have ever seen . . . Mackintosh's combination of unity in the whole with alienation in the parts is unique, masterly and profoundly disturbing.'

HITCHCOCK, Henry-Russell
Art nouveau architecture in *Art Nouveau: Art and Design at the Turn of the Century*, pp. 122-47.

New York: Museum of Modern Art, 1960.
The School is seen as diverging from art nouveau, except in the ironwork on the windows (p. 141). The book was issued in conjunction with an exhibition.

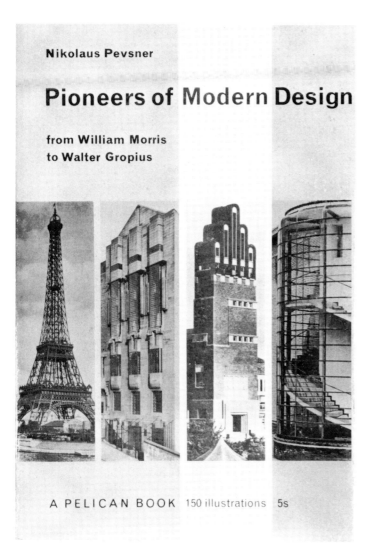

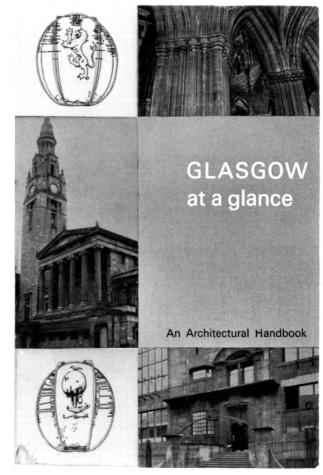

NAIRN, Ian

Glasgow and Cumbernauld New Town II.

The Listener, vol. 64, no 1650, 10 November 1960, pp. 830-3.
Contains a short, delightful, description of the School on p. 831.

PEVSNER, Nikolaus

Pioneers of Modern Design: from William Morris to Walter Gropius.

Harmondsworth: Penguin Books, 1960, 254 pp.
Contains a discussion of Mackintosh on pp. 166-75, with an analysis of the building of which there are 3 illustrations. A revised edition of *Pioneers of the Modern Movement* of 1936 (q.v.), the 2nd edn. of which was published by the Museum of Modern Art, New York, 1949.

1961   BLISS, Douglas Percy

Charles Rennie Mackintosh and Glasgow School of Art.

Glasgow: Glasgow School of Art, 1961, 24 pp.
A short treatment of the School building and its architect, with 63 illustrations including plans and elevations of the edifice as completed. Text in English with a summary in French and Italian.

1962   BANHAM, Reyner

Age of the Masters: a Personal View of Modern Architecture.

London: Architectural Press, 1962, 170 pp.
The School is discussed, on pp. 10-12, as a transitional work, between older styles and modernism. There are 2 illustrations.

SCHMUTZLER, Robert

Art Nouveau.

New York: Abrams, 1962, 322 pp.
Glasgow School of Art is discussed on pp. 241-2. There are 3 illustrations.

1964   ARCHITECTS JOURNAL

Glasgow's historic buildings: Charles Rennie Mackintosh.

Architects Journal, 6 May 1964, pp. 1019-23.
Illustrated article.

1965   BETJEMAN, John

Art belongs to Glasgow.

Weekend Telegraph, Supplement no 33, 7 May 1965, pp. 32, 35 and 36.
Does not discuss the School but has 2 illustrations of it.

YOUNG, Andrew McLaren and DOAK, A. M. (eds.)
Glasgow at a Glance: an Architectural Handbook.

Glasgow: Collins, 1965, 112 pp.
Well-illustrated historical survey of Glasgow buildings with descriptive notes. Glasgow School of Art is no 146. The entry has 12 illustrations.

WORSDALL, Francis
Prophet without honour.

Scots Magazine, vol. 83, no 6, September 1965, pp. 513-19.
Brief biography with some mention of Art School and 2 illustrations of exterior.

1967 RUBINO, Luciano
La mano di Mackintosh.

L'Architettura Cronache e Storia, no 139, May 1967, pp. 60-4 and no 140, June 1967, pp. 130-4.
Two articles on details of the Art School building. The first article has 13 illustrations, including plans; the second is mostly concerned with the Library and has 12 illustrations.

1968 BARNES, H. Jefferson
Some Examples of Furniture by Charles Rennie Mackintosh in the Glasgow School of Art Collection.

Glasgow: Glasgow School of Art, 1968, 68 pp.
Notes, photographs and measured drawings in the Glasgow School of Art Collection.

BARNES, H. Jefferson
Some Examples of Ironwork and Metalwork by Charles Rennie Mackintosh at Glasgow School of Art.

Glasgow: Glasgow School of Art, 1968, 68 pp.
Photographs, notes and some drawings of the ironwork.

GOLDBLATT, John
The genius out of his time/photographs by John Goldblatt.

Sunday Times Magazine, 27 October 1968, pp. 42-5.
The subject is Mackintosh. A collection of photographs of his work, of which 8 depict the School.

GOMME, Andor and WALKER, David M.
Architecture of Glasgow.

London: Lund Humphries, 1968, 320 pp.

An excellent historical survey of the architecture of Glasgow. Mackintosh and the Art School are covered in pp. 214-21. There are 7 photographs of the School.

HELLIER, Henry
Odd man out.

Scottish Art Review, Special number, vol. 11, no 4, 1968, pp. 18-21.
An article on Newbery's painting of the Building Committee, and on the Board Room which the work portrays and where it is hung. There are 7 illustrations.

MacDONALD, Ian
Charles Rennie Mackintosh, 1868-1928: his Buildings in and around Glasgow.

Glasgow: Glasgow District Council with C. R. Mackintosh Centenary Committee, 1968, illustrated folder.

MacLEOD, Robert
Charles Rennie Mackintosh.

London: Country Life Books, 1968, 160 pp.
Excellent treatment of Mackintosh's work in the context of his expressed ideas and those of his contemporaries and predecessors. The School is on pp. 46-61 and 120-40, with 32 illustrations.

PEVSNER, Nikolaus
Studies in Art, Architecture and Design, vol. 2: Victorian and after.

London: Thames & Hudson, 1968, 288 pp.
Contains an English translation, on pp. 152-75 of '*C. R. Mackintosh*' originally published in Italian in 1950 (q.v.).

PEVSNER, Nikolaus
The Sources of Modern Architecture and Design.

London: Thames & Hudson, 1968, 216 pp.
Discusses and illustrates the Art School on pp. 132-7, 5 illustrations.

WORSDALL, Francis
Charles Rennie Mackintosh, 1868-1928.

Scottish Field, August 1968, pp. 9-15.
Includes a description of the School with 6 illustrations.

WALKER, David M.
Charles Rennie Mackintosh.

Architectural Review, vol. 144, no 861, November 1968,
pp. 355-63.
Mackintosh and the Art School are seen against the
background of his predecessors and contemporaries in
Scottish and English architecture. Possible sources for his
buildings are indicated.

YOUNG, Andrew McLaren

Charles Rennie Mackintosh (1868-1928): architecture, design
and painting.

Edinburgh: Edinburgh Festival Society Ltd, 1968, 98 pp.
The centenary exhibition. Glasgow School of Art features at
catalogue numbers 114-128 and there are 14 illustrations
including plans and photographs.

1969 BANHAM, Reyner
The Architecture of the Well-Tempered Environment.

London: Architectural Press, 1969, 295 pp.
The plenum heating system, installed throughout the building
from 1897 onwards, is mentioned on pp. 84-6, in the context
of a discussion of two later buildings, by different architects
exploiting the same system. It is illustrated by a photograph
and a plan, incorrectly dated 1904.

HESSISCHEN LANDESMUSEUM, Darmstadt
Charles Rennie Mackintosh, 1868-1928.

Darmstadt: Hessischen Landesmuseum, 1969, 134 pp.
Selected from the 1968 Edinburgh Festival exhibition. The Art
School is featured on pp. 95-110 and is covered by 15
illustrations. Introduction in English with main text in
German.

MUSEUM DES 20 JAHRHUNDERTS. Schweizergarten,
Vienna

Charles Rennie Mackintosh.

Vienna: Museum des 20 Jahrhunderts, 1969, 52 pp.
This exhibition was transferred to Vienna from Darmstadt.
Text in German.

1971 YOUNG, Andrew McLaren and DOAK, A. M. (eds.)
Glasgow at a Glance.

Glasgow: Collins, rev. edn., 1971.
Later edition of the work published in 1965 (q.v.).

1973 ALISON, Filippo
C. R. Mackintosh.

Casabella, vol. 327, no 380-1, August-September 1973,
pp. 33-42.
Discussion of the Art School Library with plans, sections, an
axonometric and details. Text in Italian and English.

BEDFORD, June and DAVIES, Ivor
Remembering Charles Rennie Mackintosh: a recorded
interview with Mrs Mary Sturrock.

Connoisseur, vol. 183, no 738, August 1973, pp. 280-8.
Memories by Newbery's daughter of Mackintosh, the opening
of the School, and his antipathy to Continental art nouveau.

SPENCER, Isobel
Francis Newbery and the Glasgow style.

Apollo, October 1973, pp. 286-93.
Newbery's part in the building of the School is discussed.
Contains an illustration of his group portrait of the Building
Committee.

WALKER, David M.
The early work of Charles Rennie Mackintosh, in PEVSNER,
N. and RICHARDS, J. M., *The Anti-Rationalists*, pp. 116-35.

London: Architectural Press, 1973, 210 pp.
A reprint of the article which appeared in the *Architectural
Review* in November 1968 (q.v.).

1975 ASLANOGLU, Inci
Glasgow Sanat ve Mimarlik Okulu ve Charles Rennie
Mackintosh.

METU, Journal of the Faculty of Architecture, Ankara, vol. 1, no 1,
Spring 1975, pp. 23-30.
Discussion of Art School with 13 illustrations. Text in Turkish
with English summary.

NUTTGENS, Patrick
A full life and an honest place,
in CLIFTON-TAYLOR, Alec (and others), *The Spirit of the Age*,
pp. 189-213.

London: British Broadcasting Corporation, 1975, 240 pp.
The book is a collection of essays on the history of British
architecture, based on a BBC television series. The School is
dealt with in the context of the Arts and Crafts movement on
pp. 200-6, with 5 illustrations.

OPEN UNIVERSITY
History of Architecture and Design, 1890-1939, units 3-4: Art Nouveau, 1890-1902.

Milton Keynes: Open University Press, 1975, 63 pp.
An excellent analysis of the Glasgow School of Art on pp. 35-8 and 44-6, with photographs, plans and elevations. The captioning of the plans of the completed building on p. 36, however, is misleading, in dating them '1897-9', which is the correct dating for the first phase only.

WALKER, David M.
Charles Rennie Mackintosh in SERVICE, Alastair (ed.), *Edwardian Architecture and its Origins,* pp. 216-35.

London: Architectural Press, 1975, 504 pp.
Similar to the text of the *Architectural Review* article of November 1968 (q.v.).

1976 HARRIS, Alison
A report on the present and future condition of the remaining buildings of Charles Rennie Mackintosh.

Glasgow: Mackintosh School of Architecture Dissertation, 1976.
Location: Glasgow School of Art Library.

MacDONALD, Ian
Charles Rennie Mackintosh, 1868-1928: his buildings in and around the city of Glasgow.

Glasgow: City of Glasgow District Council Information Bureau, 3rd edn., 1976.
Originally published in 1968 (q.v.).

WIMPENNY, Geoffrey G.
Renovation and restoration of the Glasgow School of Art.

Charles Rennie Mackintosh Society Newsletter, no 13, Autumn 1976, pp. 11-12. Describes restoration work which was being done on the building at the time.

1977 BUCHANAN, William
Der schottische Architekt und Designer Charles Rennie Mackintosh.

Du, January 1977, pp. 68-73.
Overview of Mackintosh's work, with a brief discussion of the Art School. Includes an illustration of the Library. Text in German.

ECOLE POLYTECHNIQUE FEDERALE, Zurich. Abteilung fur Architektur
Charles Rennie Mackintosh in Glasgow.

Zurich: Ecole Polytechnique Fédérale, 1977, 98 pp.
Contains plans, details, sketches and photographs of Mackintosh's work in Glasgow. Glasgow School of Art is on pp. 19-32. Introduction in German.

HOWARTH, Thomas
Charles Rennie Mackintosh and the Modern Movement.

Routledge & Kegan Paul, 2nd edn., 1977, 335 pp.
Substantially the same text and illustrations as the 1952 edition with an additional preface and revised Bibliography.

JAPAN INTERIOR DESIGN
Charles Rennie Mackintosh.

Japan Interior Design, no 220, July 1977.
Includes an essay on the Library by Filippo Alison and a set of 8 drawings of the Library, which originally appeared in *Casabella* in 1973 (q.v.). There are also many other photographs of the School. Text in Japanese.

SERVICE, Alastair
Edwardian Architecture: A Handbook to Building Design in Britain, 1890-1914.

London: Thames & Hudson, 1977, 216 pp.
The School is briefly discussed on p. 116, but the whole book is a well-illustrated survey of building at the turn of the century, and helps to set the School in its historical context. There are 2 photographs of the building.

1978 BARNES, H. Jefferson
Charles Rennie Mackintosh and Glasgow School of Art 3: Ironwork and Metalwork at Glasgow School of Art.

Glasgow: Glasgow School of Art, rev. edn., 1978, 68 pp.

COOPER, Jackie
Mackintosh Architecture: The Complete Buildings and Selected Projects.

London: Academy Editions, 1978, 111 pp.
The School is discussed in the introduction in the context of Mackintosh's theories: pp. 20-9 are devoted to the building, with a short introduction and 23 illustrations, including drawings of all four elevations, but no plans.

GLASGOW SCHOOL OF ART
Charles Rennie Mackintosh and the Glasgow School of Art:
Furniture in the School Collection.

Glasgow: Glasgow School of Art, 2nd rev. edn., 1978, 68 pp.

1979   BARNES, H. Jefferson
Charles Rennie Mackintosh and Glasgow School of Art
1: The Architecture, Exteriors and Interiors.

Glasgow: Glasgow School of Art, 1979, 65 pp.
A redesigned and revised edition of Bliss's work of 1961 (q.v.),
with many new illustrations.

BIJUTSU TECHO
Charles Rennie Mackintosh, 1868-1928.

Bijutsu Techo, Special number, vol. 31, no 449, May 1979.
Many illustrations, including 48 of the School. Text in
Japanese.

BILLCLIFFE, Roger
Charles Rennie Mackintosh: The Complete Furniture,
Furniture Drawings and Interior Designs.

Guildford: Lutterworth Press, 1979, 256 pp.
Chronological *catalogue raisonné* of Mackintosh's work in these
fields, including the work at the Art School. Copiously
illustrated.

DAVIDSON, Peter Wylie
Memories of Mackintosh.

Charles Rennie Mackintosh Society Newsletter, no 22, Summer
1979, pp. 4-6.
Extract from the unpublished autobiography of a
contemporary of Mackintosh. Offers brief views on
Mackintosh's School of Art.

FUTAGAWA, Yukio (ed.)
Charles Rennie Mackintosh: The Glasgow School of Art,
Glasgow, Scotland, Great Britain, 1897-99, 1907-09/edited and
photographed by Yukio Futagawa, text by Andrew MacMillan.

Tokyo: ADA Edita, 1979, 7 pp. text; 6 pp. plans & elevations;
27 photographs. Global Architecture series, number 49. Text
in Japanese and English.

KIRKWOOD, Colin B.
Notes on Mackintosh buildings: Glasgow School of Art, 1896.

Charles Rennie Mackintosh Society Newsletter, no 23, Autumn
1979, p 4.
Short description of renovation programme, proceeding at the
time.

RUSSELL, Frank (ed.)
Art Nouveau Architecture.

London: Academy Editions, 1979, 332 pp.
The School is discussed briefly on pp. 46-7. The architect's
attitude to art nouveau is also touched upon. There are
2 photographs of the building and a full set of elevations.

SEIBU MUSEUM OF ART, Tokyo
Charles Rennie Mackintosh Designs.

Tokyo: Seibu Museum of Art, 1979, 106 pp.
Exhibition catalogue. Includes 13 illustrations of the School.
Text in Japanese.

1980   BILLCLIFFE, Roger
Charles Rennie Mackintosh: The Complete Furniture,
Furniture Drawings and Interior Designs.

Guildford: Lutterworth Press, 2nd edn., 1980, 264 pp.

BUCHANAN, William
Japanese influence on Charles Rennie Mackintosh.

Charles Rennie Mackintosh Society Newsletter, no 25, Spring 1980,
pp. 3-6.
Contains some discussion of possible Japanese sources for
details in the School of Art.

COOPER, Jackie
Mackintosh Architecture: The Complete Buildings and
Selected Projects.

London: Academy Editions, 2nd edn., 1980, 112 pp.
Text and black and white photographs as for 1978 edn. (q.v.),
with additional colour photographs.

DAVEY, Peter
Arts and Crafts Architecture: The Search for Earthly Paradise.

London: Architectural Press, 1980, 224 pp.
The exterior of the School is discussed briefly on p. 136, with
2 illustrations.

MacMILLAN, Andrew
Charles Rennie Mackintosh: an underestimated pioneer, a mainstream forerunner.

Architectural Association Quarterly, vol. 12, 1980, pp. 4-10.
Edited and shortened version of a lecture given at an Architectural Association symposium on expressionist architecture. Mackintosh's Art School is discussed in this context and in relation to the English House movement and modernism. Includes some illustrations of the School.

OGAWA, Moriyuki
Mackintosh as architect.

Tokyo: Aibo-Shoho, 1980, 319 pp.
Illustrations include 50 of Glasgow School of Art. Text in Japanese.

1981 ARCHITECTURAL ASSOCIATION
Some Designs by Charles Rennie Mackintosh/with biographical note by Andrew MacMillan.

Architectural Association, 1981, 49 pp.
Glasgow School of Art is featured on pp. 36-41, and is also illustrated by plans and photographs.

BARNES, H. Jefferson
The Mackintosh circle part 1: the Newberys.

Charles Rennie Mackintosh Society Newsletter, no 30, Autumn 1981, pp. 7-12.
Contains useful material on Mackintosh's struggle with the Building Committee, and on the influential figure of Newbery.

FINUCCI, Maria Cristina
L'influenza del viaggio in Italia sulla formazione del linguaggio architettonico di Charles Rennie Mackintosh.

Florence: Universita Degli Studi di Firenze, Facolta di Architettura, 1981, 3 vols.
Mostly concerned with the architect's Italian tour and its influence on his work. Glasgow School of Art is discussed in vol. 2, pp. 320-75, the section being taken up, mainly, with 55 illustrations.

1982 BUCHANAN, William
The Mackintosh circle, part 2: Mackintosh, John and Jessie Keppie.

Charles Rennie Mackintosh Society Newsletter, no 32, Midsummer 1982, pp. 3-10.

Discusses Mackintosh's partner, John Keppie, who was originally regarded as architect of the Glasgow School of Art.

COLTART, William
A detailed measured study of the Glasgow School of Art.

Glasgow: Mackintosh School of Architecture Dissertation, 1982.
Concentrates on the circulation routes through the building: plans, elevations and axonometrics — 11 sheets — recording the fabric when built, and not as it existed in 1982. Also included are the author's survey notes and sketches.
Location: Glasgow School of Art Library.

CURTI, Francesca
Charles Rennie Mackintosh.

Area, vol. 2, no 6, August-September 1982, pp. 52-5.
A general discussion of Mackintosh, with 2 illustrations of the School. Text in Italian and English.

KIMURA, Hiroaki
Charles Rennie Mackintosh: architectural drawings catalogue and design analytical catalogue.

Glasgow: University of Glasgow PhD Thesis no 6563, 1982, 338 pp. & portfolio of 25 plates. Chronological catalogue of Mackintosh's architectural drawings, all of which are illustrated: Glasgow School of Art first stage, pp. 108-13 (text, pp. 28-9); second stage, pp. 225-43 (text, pp. 55-8). The design analytical catalogue explores the development of Mackintosh's design thinking and has an analysis of the Glasgow School of Art building.
Location: University of Glasgow Library.

McKEAN, Charles
Charles Rennie Mackintosh: conservation of the architect's works.

Progressive Architecture, vol. 63, no 12, December 1982, p. 31.

WALKER, Frank
Mackintosh and Art Nouveau architecture: a paper given at a symposium, 'Art design and the quality of life in turn-of-the-century Scotland (1890-1910)', at Duncan of Jordanstone College of Art.

Dundee: Duncan of Jordanstone College of Art, 1982, pp. 52-64.
A discussion of the formal and symbolic contradictions which appear in Mackintosh's work, with special reference to the Art School.

1983   COOPER, William and MOIR, Peter

A detailed measured study of the doors and doorways of the Glasgow School of Art: survey notes, sketches and measured drawings.

Glasgow: Mackintosh School of Architecture Dissertation, 1983.
Contains survey notes and a portfolio of 27 drawings.
Location: Glasgow School of Art Library.

YOUNG, Andrew McLaren and DOAK, A. M. (eds.)

Glasgow at a Glance.

London: Robert Hale, 4th edn., 1983.
Item on Art School as for previous editions of 1977 etc. (q.v.).

GLASGOW SCHOOL OF ART

Glasgow School of Art.

Glasgow School of Art, 1983, folding leaflet, 6 pp.
Information leaflet for visitors. Short guide to rooms open to public, the furniture collection and a short history of the building, with 4 illustrations.

MacLEOD, Robert

Charles Rennie Mackintosh: Architect and Artist.

London: Collins, 1983, 160 pp.
Redesigned version of 1968 edition (q.v.).

PORTEOUS, Peter and SPEAR, Paul

The Glasgow School of Art: a measured study.

Glasgow: Mackintosh School of Architecture Dissertation, 1983, 1 vol. and loose drawings.
Survey limited to 1st and 2nd floor plans and two main sections, one through Entrance Hall and Museum, the other through the Lecture Theatre and Library, observing Mackintosh's original layout.
Location: Glasgow School of Art Library.

1984   BILLCLIFFE, Roger

Mackintosh Furniture.

Cambridge: Lutterworth Press, 1984, 223 pp.
Covers the same ground as Billcliffe's *catalogue raisonné* of 1979 (q.v.), but in more condensed form.

BILLCLIFFE, Roger

Mackintosh Furniture.

Tokyo: Hoga-Shoten, 1984, 257 pp.
Text in Japanese.

BUILDING DESIGN

Mackintosh tops poll.

Building Design, no 683, 30 March 1984, p. 1.
A readers' poll voted Mackintosh the best British architect in the past 150 years and the Glasgow School of Art as the best building.

ENNIS, John

Scotland's neglected giant of architecture.

Reader's Digest, May 1984, pp. 86-91.
A general biography of Mackintosh with some quotations from present-day authorities. The Art School is mentioned and illustrated as a matter of course.

FRIEDMANN, Arnold

Glasgow revisited: design educator Arnold Friedmann encounters the work of Charles Rennie Mackintosh.

Interior Design, vol. 55, no 2, February 1984, pp. 182-5.
Impressions of the author, who spent two weeks as an exchange professor at Glasgow School of Art. Includes 8 photographs of the School.

KIMURA, Hiroaki

Charles Rennie Mackintosh/preface by Andrew MacMillan.

Process Architecture, no 50, 1984, 151 pp.
The material and treatment are much the same as in Kimura's 1982 thesis (q.v.). Excellent analysis of the School and its construction, helpfully illustrated by comparative plans and elevations showing the development of the design.

1985   CHARLES RENNIE MACKINTOSH SOCIETY NEWSLETTER

Campus competition: Glasgow School of Art.

Charles Rennie Mackintosh Society Newsletter, no 42, Winter 1985-6, p. 4.
Winning design in a competition to redesign the street environment on the north side of Mackintosh's building.

JAPAN ART & CULTURE ASSOCIATION
Charles Rennie Mackintosh.

Tokyo: Japan Art & Culture Association, 1985, 159 pp.
Contains little information on the Art School building, but a
large proportion of the exhibits were drawn from the School's
collection. The building is featured on pp. 143-5. Well
illustrated with parallel text in English and Japanese.

MacINTYRE, Lorn
Portrait of the artist as an old friend: Lorn MacIntyre talks to
Mary Sturrock.

Scotsman Magazine, vol. 5, no 10, January 1985.
An interview with Newbery's daughter, with material on her
father's association with Mackintosh and the Art School
building.

1986   BILLCLIFFE, Roger
Charles Rennie Mackintosh: The Complete Furniture,
Furniture Drawings and Interior Designs.

London: John Murray, 3rd edn., 1986, 272 pp.

1987   GOMME, Andor and WALKER, David M.
Architecture of Glasgow.

London: Lund Humphries, 2nd edn., 1987, 344 pp.

GRIGG, Jocelyn
Charles Rennie Mackintosh.

Glasgow: Richard Drew, 1987, 96 pp.
Well-illustrated introduction to Mackintosh's work, with
description of the principal features of the School.

HARRIGAN, John
A survey and report on the centrepiece of the Glasgow School
of Art.

Glasgow: Mackintosh School of Architecture Dissertation,
1987.
Discussion of this section of the building, with 12
accompanying drawings.
Location: Glasgow School of Art Library.

PINKERTON, Andrew
Keppie Henderson archives: an important source for
Mackintosh research.

Charles Rennie Mackintosh Society Newsletter, no 45, Spring 1987,
pp. 4-6.
A short discussion of the job books held by Keppie
Henderson, Architects, Glasgow.

1988   BARNES, H. Jefferson
Charles Rennie Mackintosh and Glasgow School of Art
1: The Architecture, Exteriors and Interiors.

Glasgow: Glasgow School of Art, 3rd edn., 1988, 72 pp.

CAIRNS, G. M.
Survey and analysis of the west wing of the Glasgow School of
Art.

Glasgow: Mackintosh School of Architecture Dissertation,
1988.
Contains three-dimensional sectional axonometric drawings,
showing the west wing as constructed in 1907-9. It includes an
analysis of the original warm-air heating system with
suggestions for replacement of a similar system.
Location: Glasgow School of Art Library.

NUTTGENS, Patrick
Understanding Modern Architecture.

London: Unwin Hyman, 1988, 220 pp.
Contains a chapter on Mackintosh as a master of architectural
space, with a discussion of the School on pp. 54-9, including
5 photographs of the building.

NUTTGENS, Patrick (ed.)
Mackintosh and his Contemporaries: in Europe and America.

London: John Murray, 1988, 160 pp.
The book contains papers read at a conference in Glasgow,
held in August 1983, to mark the tenth anniversary of the
Charles Rennie Mackintosh Society. Howarth discusses the
School interior on pp. 39-41, and the book contains 7
photographs of the building.

PALAZZO VICARIALE DI CERTALDO
Charles Rennie Mackintosh, 1868-1928.

Florence: Electa, 1988, 196 pp.
Glasgow School of Art is covered on pp. 74-87; well-illustrated
exhibition catalogue. Text in Italian.

APPENDIX A

THE GLASGOW SCHOOL OF ART.

Limited Competition of Architects for the Proposed New School of Art.

CONDITIONS OF COMPETITION.

1. The Building Committee appointed by the Governors of the Glasgow School of Art, invite you to submit a design for a School of Art to provide accommodation for Life; Antique; Painting; Modelling; Design and Technical Rooms; Rooms and Studios for Staff; School Museum; Retiring Rooms; Lavatories; Cloak Rooms; Offices and Store Rooms; as well as accommodation for a Resident Janitor.

2. A plan of the site, with four cross sections shewing the contours of the ground, is herewith enclosed. The building with all breaks and projections, as produced for architectural effect, must be confined within the building lines shewn on the plan. The buttresses supporting the building, at present occupied by the Glasgow Real Ice Skating Company, Limited, are shewn encroaching upon the southern building line of the site. Should any wall be built along the southern building line of the site, it must be done in such a way as not to affect, prejudicially, these said buttresses.

3. The Governors have asked Sir James King, Bart., and Sir Renny Watson to act as Assessors, with power to call in such professional aid as they may think proper, to guide them in their decision, and to advise them as to the estimates of the cost, submitted by the competitors.

4. The designs shall be illustrated by a plan of each floor, a longitudinal section, two cross sections, and three elevations, north, east and south, drawn to a scale of one-sixteenth of an inch to a foot. Perspectives are not admissible, and must not be sent in. The successful architect to provide one set of plans for the Dean of Guild Court; one set for the Science and Art Department; and one set for the Governors. This last set must show the completed building, and include a special plan of the drains.

5. All the drawings should be on sheets of plain paper, and mounted on plain stretchers, without frames. The north side of the plans should be kept towards the lower edges of the stretchers.

6. The geometrical elevations are to be in outline only, without shading or etching of any kind, except that a flat tint, of dark Indian ink, may indicate the clear opening of doors and windows, and a lighter tint the roofs and any recessed portions.

7. The accommodation on the north side should be, as far as possible, rigidly kept for class-rooms.

8. The south elevation may not have any lights in its walls, in a line with the building line, except perhaps in the upper floor.

9. The accommodation should be allocated into spaces, as follow:—

A. One Ornament Room, say 72′ × 35′ = 2520 sq. ft. lighted from the north side, to accommodate Elementary and Advanced Ornament Work; the floor space to be divisible by a moveable partition. This room should be contiguous to a corridor, or other place, where casts may be hung or stored.

B. One Lecture Theatre, say 35′ × 32′ = 1120 sq. ft., contiguous to room A, and furnished with the necessary accommodation. Adjoining the lecture platform, a lecturer's room may be provided for the storage of lecture material.

C. One Design Room, say 49′ × 35′ = 1715 sq. ft. This room need not necessarily be lighted from the north.

D. One School Library and Reading Room with a floor space of from 1000 to 1200 sq. ft. This room should adjoin and communicate with room C.

E. Rooms for Architectural Study—two in number. (1) Building Construction and Architectural Drawing Room, say 49′ × 35′ = 1715 sq. ft. This floor space to be divisible by a moveable partition. (2) Lecture Room, say 40′ × 23′ = 920 sq. ft., having arrangements similar to those required under B. These two rooms should adjoin each other.

F. Rooms for Still Life and Flower Painting—two in number. (1) For Advanced and Elementary Still Life, say 72′ × 35′ = 2520 sq. ft. divisible by moveable partitions. (2) Flower Painting Room, say 40′ × 23′ = 920 sq. ft. Room (1) should be lighted entirely from the north side; Room (2) may be lighted from the ends or by a north top-light, and should have attached to it, a conservatory, with an exposure to the sun, in which plants and flowers, when not in use, may be kept.

G. Antique Rooms—two in number. (1) Advanced Antique Room, say 63′ × 35′ = 2200 sq. ft., with a depth from the windows of not more than 35 feet. (2) Elementary Antique Room, say 49′ × 35′ = 1715 sq. ft. with a depth from the windows of not more than 35 feet. These two rooms must be lighted from the north by large square headed windows, the tops of which (carried up in a dormer if necessary, but not returned upon the roof) should be at a height above the floor, equal to ¾ the depth of the room. These windows should be free from mullions and small panes, and should be in the length of the room.

H. Life Rooms—two in number. (1) Male Life Room, say 62′ × 35′ = 2170 sq. ft., and with a depth similar to that stated for rooms under G.; (2) Female Life Room, say 43′ × 35′ = 1500 sq. ft., and with a similar depth to (1) H. The conditions of lighting for these rooms, must be exactly the same as those required for rooms under G. Small Dressing-spaces for the life models, should either be accommodated in or attached to these rooms, and the hot coil should be near the throne. It is desirable that the rooms under G, or under H, be so arranged, as to permit of their being thrown into one, on special occasions.

I. Modelling Rooms—three in number. (1) Ornament Modelling Room, say 40′ × 35′ = 1400 sq. ft.; (2) Antique Modelling Room, say 40′ × 23′ = 920 sq. ft.; and (3) A Life Modelling Room, say 40′ × 22′ = 880 sq. ft., and with either a top or a north light. These rooms should be adjacent to and communicating with each other, and the same accommodation as under H, should be provided in room (3) for the life models. Access to these rooms may be got from the east or west side street by a service door, in order that modelling material be not carried through the building.

K. Technical Studios for Stained Glass and China Painting; Metal Work; Wood Carving; Needle Work. Accommodation should be made for these in a room or rooms having a total floor space of about 1500 to 2000 sq. ft., and divisible into smaller rooms, by means of partitions. The Metal Work Room should be situated, where the noise made by the workers should not be disturbing to other students working in the vicinity. A north light is not needed for this class of work.

L. One Headmaster's Room with Studio attached. These should be in a central position on the upper floor, and should have a total floor space of about 850 sq. ft. The Studio should be lighted from the north side.

M. Rooms for Staff—three in number. (1) Room for male Teachers with a floor space of about 400 sq. ft.; and (2) one of smaller size for female Teachers. These should in each case be provided with Lavatory accommodation; (3) Studio accommodation for male and female Staff, with a floor space of about 800 to 1000 sq. ft., and having a north light.

N. One Janitor's Office, having floor space of about 300 sq. ft. This Office must be placed so as to command all ingress and egress at the main entrance. It should also afford accommodation for the sale of School material.

O. One Secretary's Office and Board Room to have a floor space of about 900 sq. ft. This should be on the upper floor and may be ceiled low enough to admit of the presence of studios above, for the staff. These studios should have a north top-light.

P. One room for the reception, storage, and packing of Students' works. This should have a floor space of about 700 sq. ft.; may be in an unimportant part of the building, and may be lighted from any side. This room should be placed near to, or adjoining, the heating apparatus room and the lift.

Q. Luncheon Rooms—two in number. One each for male and female Students should be provided, with a total floor space of about 800 sq. ft.

R. One Heating Chamber and Coal Store, placed near the centre of the building, and arranged so that access to the street can readily be had, for the purposes of service.

S. One Box Store for packing-cases, forms, seats, and School plant generally, when not in use. This might be contiguous to room P.

T. Separate Cloak-Rooms and Lavatories must be provided for male and female Students. The females' accommodation should be in a different part of the building from that allotted to male Students.

10. All rooms for study should be not less than 16 feet high to the wall plate, if ceiled flat, or 14 feet high to the wall plate, if ceiled to the collar beams or the common rafters. Rooms that are top-lighted, should, in all cases, be ceiled to the common rafters, in order to give increased height, and all tie beams or other heavy roof timbering should be avoided. The sills of the windows in class rooms should be not more than 3′ 6″ to 4′ from the floors.

11. All Class-Rooms, on any floor, should, as far as possible, communicate with each other directly, as well as be entered upon from the corridors. The staircase should be at the centre of the building and should give access to all rooms, without passing through rooms. Arrangements should be made for a lift.

12. It is suggested that the Life and Antique Rooms be on the upper floors; that the Painting Rooms be partly on the upper floor and partly on the ground floor; that the Ornament, Design, and Architectural Rooms be on the ground floor; and that the Modelling and Technical Rooms be in the basement.

13. The rooms should be well ventilated by the admission of fresh air, without causing draughts, and by the extraction of vitiated air by means of shafts carried up above the roofs.

14. The warming of the rooms will be by hot water, or other apparatus, and the corridors must receive equal consideration with the class rooms. The lighting of the School is proposed to be by electricity.

15. The corridors should be not less than 10 feet wide. They should be well lighted and have good wall spaces, so that casts and other exhibits may be arranged in chronological order. Particularly should these corridors be made available for the periodical Exhibition of Students' Works. The School Museum need not be a special room, but might be a feature in connection with the staircase.

16. A residence for the Janitor may be included, with access from the side street. 2500 feet or 3000 feet of floorage may be allowed for this, and the usual accommodation given.

17. The conditions set forth by the Science and Art Department must receive attention. These are to be found on pp. 116 and 117 of the current Art Directory revised to June, 1895.

18. Each set of drawings must be accompanied by a concise statement detailing the materials suggested, and giving the net cubical contents of the proposed building, calculated from the bottom of the footings, and including all walls; partitions; roofs; chimney stacks or ventilating shafts, or other special features; with a schedule of the dimensions on which such cubic contents are based.

19. The following extract from a Minute of a Meeting of the Governors, held in the School of Art, on Monday, March 16th, 1896, must be considered as absolutely binding on the Architects invited to compete :—

"That the sum of £14,000 be the limit given as the total cost of the building, "inclusive of lighting and heating and ventilating apparatus, draining, paving, and "altering streets ready for occupation ; also of Architects', Measurer's, and Clerk of "Works' fees, but exclusive of retaining wall and painting."

And further—

"That if on the measurement of any competing Architect's plan, the sum named "be exceeded by 10%, that plan to be excluded from the competition."

20. The Governors would desire that Architects permit themselves as much freedom of judgment as is compatible with the conditions as herein set forth, and it is further their desire that any suggestions, made herein, be not regarded by Architects as final. What is required, is a building with class rooms conveniently arranged and well lighted.

21. No premiums are offered competing Architects. The successful Architect shall receive a commission of 5 per cent. on the total cost of the building, exclusive of furniture and Measurer's and Clerk of Works' fees.

22. Each set of drawings must be marked with a seal, sign, or motto, and be accompanied with a sealed envelope, enclosing a replica of this same seal, sign, or motto, together with the Architect's name and address.

23. All designs must be sent in on *Tuesday, September 15th, 1896*, addressed— "The Secretary, The Glasgow School of Art, 3 Rose Street, Glasgow."

By order of the Governors,

E. R. CATTERNS, *Secretary.*

THE GLASGOW SCHOOL OF ART,
June, 1896.

The Glasgow School of Art,

PLAN AND SECTIONS OF SITE FOR THE PROPOSED NEW SCHOOL.

—PLAN—

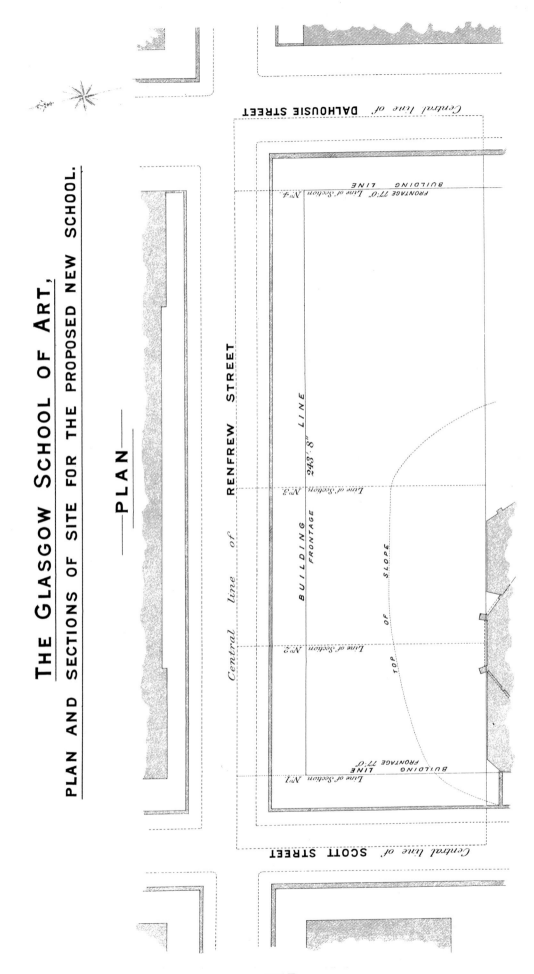

SECTIONS

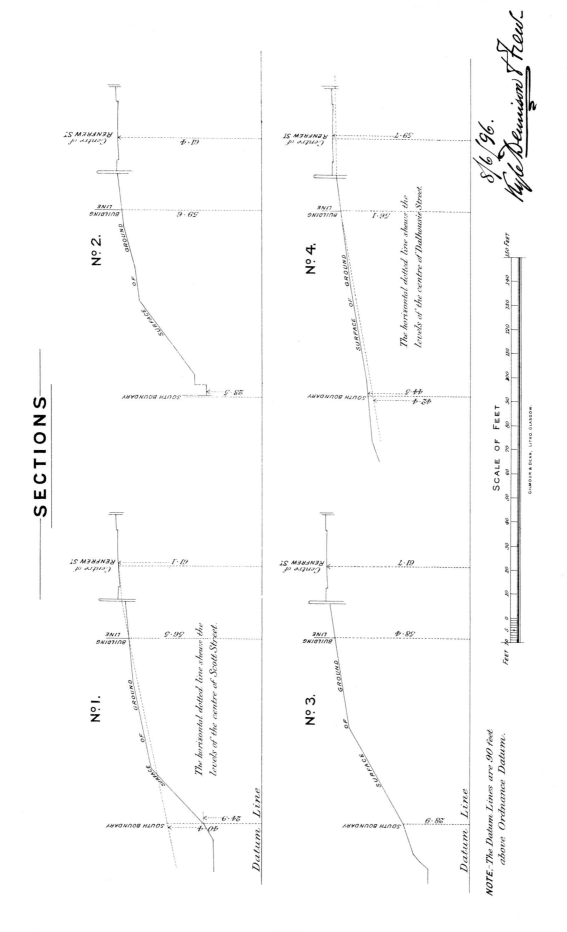

Nº 1.

The horizontal dotted line shews the levels of the centre of Scott Street.

Datum Line

Nº 2.

Nº 3.

Datum Line

Nº 4.

The horizontal dotted line shews the levels of the centre of Dalhousie Street.

NOTE.—The Datum Lines are 90 feet above Ordnance Datum.

SCALE OF FEET

GILMOUR & DEAN, LITHO. GLASGOW.

8/6/96.

THE
GLASGOW SCHOOL OF ART.

CONDITIONS

OF THE

COMPETITION OF ARCHITECTS

FOR THE

PROPOSED NEW SCHOOL OF ART.

THE SCHOOL OF ART,
3 ROSE STREET,
GLASGOW.

EDW. R. CATTERNS,
Secretary.

APPENDIX B

*Further reading on the Visual Arts
in Glasgow at the turn of the century*

ARCHITECTURE

Andrew McLaren Young and A. M. Doak (eds.), *Glasgow at a Glance*, Collins, 1965, 1971; Robert Hale, 1977, 1983.

Andor Gomme and David M. Walker, *Architecture of Glasgow*, Lund Humphries, 1968; 2nd edn., Lund Humphries with John Smith, 1987.

David M. Walker, 'Sir John James Burnet' and 'The Partnership of James Salmon and John Gaff Gillespie' in Alastair Service (ed.), *Edwardian Architecture and its Origins*, Architectural Press, 1975.

Ronald McFadzean, *The Life and Work of Alexander Thomson*, Routledge & Kegan Paul, 1979.

Frank Worsdall, *Victorian City: A Selection of Glasgow's Architecture*, Richard Drew, 1982.

ART COLLECTIONS

Richard Marks, *Burrell: Portrait of a Collector*, Richard Drew, 1983; 2nd (rev.) edn., 1988.

Alasdair Auld *et al*, *Glasgow Art Gallery and Museum: The Building and the Collection*, Collins/Glasgow Museums & Art Galleries, 1987.

EMBROIDERY

Fiona Macfarlane and Elizabeth Arthur, *Glasgow School of Art Embroidery 1894-1920*, Catalogue, Glasgow Museums & Art Galleries, 1980.

Margaret Swain, *Scottish Embroidery*, Batsford, 1986.

FURNITURE BY MACKINTOSH

H. Jefferson Barnes, *Furniture in the School Collection*, Glasgow School of Art, 1968 and 1978.

Filippo Alison, *Charles Rennie Mackintosh as a Designer of Chairs*, Warehouse, 1974.

Roger Billcliffe, *Charles Rennie Mackintosh: The Complete Furniture, Furniture Drawings & Interior Designs*, Lutterworth, 1979; 3rd edn., John Murray, 1986.

GLASGOW STYLE

Gerald and Celia Larner, *The Glasgow Style*, Paul Harris, 1979.

Brian Blench, Rosemary Watt, Elizabeth Arthur, Juliet Kinchin, Jonathan Kinghorn and Fiona McNaught, *The Glasgow Style 1890-1920*, Catalogue, Glasgow Museums & Art Galleries, 1984.

GRAPHIC DESIGN

John Russell Taylor, *The Art Nouveau Book in Britain*, Methuen, 1966.

H. Jefferson Barnes, Joan Hughson, and Cordelia Oliver, *Jessie M. King and E. A. Taylor: Illustrator and Designer*, Paul Harris & Sotheby's Belgravia, 1977.

Chris S. Seaton, 'The Book Designs of Talwin Morris (1865-1911)' in Alexander Fenton (ed.), *Review of Scottish Culture 2*, John Donald & National Museums of Scotland, 1986, pp. 13-17.

Robert Gibbs, 'Scottish Commercial Bookbindings at the turn of the 20th Century' in *Aspects of Scottish Decorative Art in the Twentieth Century*, Year Book of the Scottish Society for Art History, 1988.

PAINTING

William Buchanan, *Mr Henry and Mr Hornel Visit Japan*, Catalogue, Scottish Arts Council, 1978.

Roger Billcliffe, *The Glasgow Boys*, John Murray, 1985.

PHOTOGRAPHY

William Buchanan, 'James Craig Annan: Brave Days in Glasgow' in Mark Haworth-Booth (ed.), *The Golden Age of British Photography 1839-1900*, Aperture/Victoria & Albert Museum, 1984.

STAINED GLASS

Michael Donnelly, *Glasgow Stained Glass*, Glasgow Museums & Art Galleries, 1981.

WOMEN ARTISTS

Ailsa Tanner, *West of Scotland Women Artists*, Catalogue, Helensburgh & District Art Club, 1976.

Elizabeth Bird, 'Threading the Beads: Women in Art in Glasgow, 1870-1920' in *Uncharted Lives*, Pressgang, 1983.

Jude Burkhauser, Elizabeth Bird and Ailsa Tanner, *Glasgow Girls: Women in the Art School 1880-1920*, Catalogue, Glasgow School of Art, 1988.

PHOTOGRAPHY

Specially commissioned photographs:
11, 14, 15, 16, 17, 18, 19, 22, 23(a),
28, 29, 37, 42, 43, 48, 49, 50, 54, 59,
60, 61, 71, 72, 73, 81, 85, 86, 87, 92,
97, 100, 103, 108, 112, 116, 142, 147,
148, 150, 151, 152, 154, 159, and on
pages 4, 6, 118, 203, 214, 224 Ralph
Burnett;
80, James Carney.

Existing photographs:
21, 46, 72, 99, 102, Ralph Burnett;
23(b), 75, James Murray;
41, Bryan & Shear;
53, 101, Douglas Corrance;
63, William Buchanan;
123, James Macaulay;
141, Tony Jones;
155, 162, Michael Graham.

The photographers of 47, 76, 106,
160 and 161 are not known. Should
they be traced acknowledgement will
be gladly made when the book
reprints.

It has proved impossible to trace the
owners of the items reproduced in
136, 137.

170
J. Craig Annan
MARGARET MACDONALD MACKINTOSH
c. 1903
Photograph
Taken in the drawing room, 120 Mains Street,
Glasgow
William Buchanan